P9-CKR-841

CHILDREN'S PARTY CAKES

SUE ALDRIDGE

I dedicate this book to my family:

Wayne, Chevaune and Megan, who have been my inspiration and most honest critics.

First published in 1998 by
New Holland (Publishers) Ltd
London • Cape Town • Sydney • Singapore

24 Nutford Place
London W1H 6DQ, United Kingdom

80 McKenzie Street
Cape Town 8001, South Africa

3/2 Aquatic Drive
Frenchs Forest, NSW 2086, Australia

ISBN 1 85974 058 8 (p/b)
ISBN 1 85368 986 6 (h/b)

EDITOR Thea Coetzee
DESIGNER Mandy McKay
COVER DESIGN Petal Palmer
DESIGN ASSISTANT Lellyn Creamer
PHOTOGRAPHER Sally Chance
STYLIST Sue Aldridge
ILLUSTRATOR Darren McLean

Reproduction by Hirt & Carter Cape (Pty) Ltd
Printed and bound by Times Offset (M) Sdn Bhd

ACKNOWLEDGEMENTS

My thanks go to photographer Sally Chance who was such fun to work with and yet so professional; to David Leeney for his assistance with earlier photography; to Sandy Bagpie and Robyne Cackett for presentation of the text; to Christine Edges for her assistance with the typing; to Warren and Ellen Zolty of The Baking Tin in Durban for all their advice; and to Rosy Mabaso and Cyril Nala for all their help behind the scenes.

Contents

Introduction

The aim of this book is to provide a varied selection of birthday cakes to those entrusted with organizing that all important annual event – 'My Birthday'. The excitement and anticipation of each child for this special day can be mirrored by the fun in creating the birthday cake, the memory of which will last a lifetime.

The birthday cakes in this book have been designed to appeal primarily to the visual and taste senses of children. Bearing this in mind, decorations on cakes include plenty of sweets – an obvious choice when you consider the incredible variety now available at specialist sweet shops. I have only resorted to the home-made variety when unable to find a ready-made alternative at these outlets.

I have tried a fresh approach to children's birthday cakes by using choux pastry and ice-cream besides the traditional Madeira and sponge cake bases. Most of the cakes are iced with butter icing, which is easier to work with and which I believe children generally prefer. Apart from the sweets used for decorating, the cakes also feature easy piped work and even fresh fruit for the health conscious.

Each cake has detailed instructions for construction, icing and decoration, and for your convenience there are reference sections containing tried-and-tested basic recipes and techniques. In addition, there are several templates at the back of the book to assist you in shaping the cakes.

Whether you are a cook of some experience or have never iced a cake before, you will find this an invaluable, practical guide, as most of the cakes are very easy to prepare. I have, however, added a few more challenging ones for those who like to experiment.

I hope you, your children and their friends will enjoy paging through this book before choosing a cake for that special birthday. The limitless variations in cake decoration, I am certain, will fire your enthusiasm to experiment and I hope you will have as much fun and pleasure as I have had in creating this book for you.

Sue Aldridge

General Tips on Baking

Good cakes can only be produced in accurate ovens that conduct heat evenly and efficiently, and by using quality ingredients and baking equipment.

1. Baking tin moulds, especially for children's cakes, can be hired from cake icing shops.
2. Always check the position of the oven shelf, set the oven temperature, and line and grease the tins before assembling your ingredients. This will ensure that the mixed batter does not deteriorate while you wait for the oven to reach the correct temperature.
3. For the best results ensure that the ingredients are at room temperature. These include milk, butter and eggs, which should be removed from the refrigerator at least one hour before baking.
4. Break and then separate the eggs when they are cold, but leave them to reach room temperature before using them.
5. Always sift the flour, salt, baking powder or cocoa powder onto kitchen paper towelling before adding to the other ingredients. This technique makes the sifting process easier (due to the larger surface area of the paper) and more accurate (as the dry ingredients are less likely to stick to the paper than to a plate). Sifting the flour from a fair height also serves to aerate and lighten a cake.
6. Once you have added the bicarbonate of soda or baking powder to the cake mix, you should place the cake in the oven as soon as possible.
7. Always replace the lid of the baking powder tin tightly immediately after use. This prevents the release of carbon dioxide, which causes the baking powder to be less effective in future baking. To maintain the effectiveness of the baking powder, it is advisable to buy it in smaller quantities and replace it more often.
8. Never knock the cake tins before placing the cake mix in the oven. Place tins gently onto the prepared rack in the oven, unless a thermofan oven is being used, in which case you may use any of the racks.
9. Never allow cake tins to touch in the oven or to touch the sides of the oven – the cake will burn in this area due to conducted heat.
10. Never open the oven door to check the cake until three-quarters of the cooking time has elapsed. Open the oven door only very slightly when inspecting the cake to avoid a rush of cold air into the oven and the subsequent collapse of the cake.
11. Test butter cakes with a skewer (if the cake is ready, the skewer will come out of the centre of the cooked cake clean), and sponge cakes using the finger test (when pressing the cooked cake lightly with the finger, no dent should be left in the cake – it should spring back into position when the finger is released).
12. Always leave cakes in the tin for 5–10 minutes before gently loosening the sides with a smooth-edged knife. Invert onto a wire rack. Remove the non-stick paper carefully without tearing the cake. Turn the cake back onto its right side using another wire rack (if it is left to cool top side down, the top crust will stick to the rack). Leave to cool in a position where there is no draught, as a sudden change in temperature will cause the cake to shrivel slightly.
13. Make sure cakes are completely cold before icing them, to prevent the icing from melting. Store cakes in airtight containers only when completely cold.
14. Butter cakes freeze well if properly wrapped and sealed in strong plastic. The birthday cake should ideally be baked the day before it is iced to allow the sponge to be firmer and less likely to crumble when sections are removed for shaping or when it is iced.

Basic Madeira Cake

This is a rich, long-lasting cake that is easy to cut and shape.

INSTRUCTIONS

1. Position the shelf in the middle of the oven, ensuring that there is an equal distance above and below the baking tin.
2. Set the oven at 180 °C (350 °F).
3. Line the base of the baking tin with non-stick baking paper and grease the sides well with softened butter, margarine or a non-stick cooking spray.

INGREDIENTS

750 ml (375 g, 12 oz, 3 cups) flour
15 ml (1 tbsp) baking powder
Pinch of salt
250 g (8 oz) butter or margarine
375 ml (300 g, 10 oz, 1½ cups) caster sugar
10 ml (2 tsp) vanilla essence
4 large eggs (at room temperature)
250 ml (8 fl oz, 1 cup) milk (food colouring may be added to this by skewer or by dropper)

METHOD

1. Sift the flour, baking powder and salt onto kitchen paper towel.
2. Soften the butter, using a wooden spoon or electric beater. Gradually add the caster sugar and beat the mixture until it is pale yellow, light and fluffy.
3. Add the vanilla essence, then the eggs (beaten individually) one at a time, adding 15 ml (1 tbsp) flour for each egg to avoid curdling.
4. Using a metal spoon or spatula, gently fold the remaining flour and milk into the mixture. Keep the mixing down to a minimum – it is merely to mix the ingredients together evenly into a soft consistency.
5. Pour the mixture into the prepared baking tin, smooth the surface and bake for about 40–45 minutes (this depends on the shape and thickness of the cake – refer to the chart below as a guideline). Perform the skewer test when you think the cake is ready.
6. Leave the cake in the baking tin for 10 minutes, then gently loosen the edges with a sharp knife and turn it onto a wire rack. Remove the non-stick baking paper.
7. Never leave the cake upside down to cool. Turn it over with its top side facing up and then leave it to cool on the wire rack in a position in the kitchen where there is no draught.
8. Only ice the cake when it is completely cold.

VARIATIONS

Chocolate cake: replace 75 ml (37.5 g, 1¼ oz, ⅓ cup, 6 tbsp) of the flour with cocoa powder.
Orange cake: replace the vanilla essence with about 20 ml (4 tsp) grated orange rind and also substitute 250 ml (8 fl oz, 1 cup) squeezed and strained orange juice for the milk.

DEEP CAKE TIN SIZE	COOKING TIME	QUANTITY OF MIXTURE	NUMBER OF EGGS
15 cm (6 in)	35–40 mins	½	2
18 cm (7 in)	40–45 mins	¾	3
20 cm (8 in)	45 mins	1	4
23 cm (9 in)	45–50 mins	1¼	5
25 cm (10 in)	50–55 mins	1½	6

Oil Sponge Cake

This is my favourite recipe for children's birthday cakes. It is very easy to make, lasts for at least four to five days, freezes well and is not difficult to shape. In addition, it has an excellent texture and taste.

INSTRUCTIONS

1. Use the middle shelf of the oven to bake.
2. Set the oven at 180 °C (350 °F).
3. Prepare the baking tin by lining the base with non-stick baking paper and then greasing the sides very well with softened butter or margarine, or use a non-stick cooking spray.

INGREDIENTS

375 ml (12 fl oz, 1½ cups) milk (or water or half and half)
125 ml (4 fl oz, ½ cup) oil
4 large eggs
400 ml (320 g, 11 oz, 1⅗ cups) caster sugar
5 ml (1 tsp) vanilla essence
Food colouring (optional)
625 ml (310 g, 10 oz, 2½ cups) flour, sifted
2 ml (½ tsp) salt
20 ml (4 tsp) baking powder

METHOD

1. Boil the milk (or water) and oil together in a saucepan. Leave to cool.
2. Beat the eggs in a large bowl, and gradually add the caster sugar until the mixture is pale yellow and frothy. Add the vanilla essence and food colouring (if using).
3. Using a metal spoon or spatula, fold half the sifted flour and salt into the egg mixture followed by half the boiled milk (water) and oil mixture. Blend lightly, then add the remaining flour and the milk (water) and oil mixture, stirring well to remove all the lumps, but maintaining a soft, foamy consistency.
4. Lastly, add the sifted baking powder, folding it in gently but thoroughly to ensure an even distribution of the baking powder throughout the sponge mixture.
5. Pour into the prepared baking tin leaving the top quarter of the tin free for rising. Bake 25–30 minutes (depending on the size and shape of the cake – refer to the chart below as a guideline) until no dent is left when doing the finger test. When using this recipe for a deep shape, for example the doll's skirt or loaf tin, test centre with a skewer to check that it is cooked.
6. Leave the sponge cake to cool in the baking tin for 5–10 minutes. Gently loosen the sides with a sharp knife and turn it over onto a wire rack (remember to remove the paper), then turn the cake back onto its right side to cool completely on the wire rack. Make sure your wire rack is nowhere near a draught.

VARIATION

Chocolate cake: Add 125 ml (50 g, 2 oz, ½ cup) cocoa powder to the milk (water) and oil mixture and simmer. Use 500 ml (250 g, 8 oz, 2 cups) instead of 625 ml (310 g, 10 oz, 2½ cups) flour for this recipe.

DEEP CAKE TIN SIZE	COOKING TIME	QUANTITY OF MIXTURE	NUMBER OF EGGS
15 cm (6 in)	20 mins	½	2
18 cm (7 in)	20–25 mins	¾	3
20 cm (8 in)	25–30 mins	1	4
23 cm (9 in)	30–35 mins	1¼	5
25 cm (10 in)	35–40 mins	1½	6
Loaf Tin (11 x 4 in)	30–35 mins	1¼	5

Swiss Roll

Traditionally swiss rolls are made without butter or margarine and therefore do not last longer than two to three days.

INSTRUCTIONS

1. Use the second shelf of the oven.
2. Set the oven at 200 °C (400 °F).
3. Use a 23 x 30 cm (9 x 12 in) baking tray.
4. To line the baking tray with non-stick baking paper, trace the base of the baking tray onto the non-stick baking paper. Next, add 4 cm (1½ in) all the way around your tracing. Slash the corners to the tracing line corners and fit the paper into the baking tray.

INGREDIENTS

3 large eggs (at room temperature)
90 ml (90 g, 3 oz, ⅓ cup) caster sugar
180 ml (90 g, 3 oz, ¾ cup) flour
5 ml (1 tsp) baking powder
Smooth jam, for example apricot jam

METHOD

1. Whisk the eggs together, and then gradually add the caster sugar and beat until the mixture is light and creamy. The mixture should leave a trail when the whisk is lifted out of it.
2. Sift the flour and baking powder together and very gently fold this into the egg mixture using a metal spoon or spatula.
3. Pour the mixture into the prepared baking tin and gently smooth the surface with a palette knife.
4. Bake in a hot oven for 7–10 minutes, until the sponge is golden and the sides start to shrink away from the edge of the baking tin. Perform the finger test.
5. Prepare the work surface while the swiss roll is baking, as you have to work rapidly at this stage. First lay out a sheet of non-stick baking paper (larger than the swiss roll) and sprinkle it with caster sugar. Have a large sharp knife ready for trimming the sides of the cake. Have the warmed jam (which is easier to spread than cold jam) and a palette knife ready.
6. When the swiss roll is cooked, remove it from the oven and carefully turn it out onto the non-stick baking paper. Remove the paper lining quickly and carefully, then trim the four crisp edges of the cake using the sharp knife. Spread the whole surface of the cake with the warmed jam and then roll it up firmly, using the non-stick baking paper and positioning the join at the base of the roll.
7. Allow the cake to cool completely before serving.

NOTE

Butter icing or whipped cream may be used as a filling. In this case, the hot swiss roll should be rolled with a sheet of non-stick baking paper on the inside and left to cool. When cold, carefully unroll the swiss roll, remove the paper, spread the cake with the butter icing or whipped cream filling and re-roll.

Choux Pastry

This recipe makes 18 choux pastries.

INSTRUCTIONS

1. Use the middle shelf of the oven for baking.
2. Set the oven at 200 °C (400 °F).

INGREDIENTS

50 g (1¾ oz) butter or margarine
125 ml (4 fl oz, ½ cup) water
150 ml (75 g, 2½ oz, ⅔ cup) flour, sifted
Pinch of salt
2 large eggs, beaten

METHOD

1. Bring butter and water to the boil in a saucepan.
2. Remove from heat and quickly add flour and salt.
3. Stir over low heat with a wooden spoon until the paste forms a ball and the sides of the saucepan are clean.
4. Allow the paste to cool slightly, then place it in an electric mixing bowl and turn the beaters on to a low speed. Gradually add the beaten eggs to the mixture.
5. Beat well and increase speed to high for a minute. Spoon or pipe the choux pastry onto the lightly greased baking tray, allowing space for expansion.
6. Bake 20–30 minutes, depending on size and shape.
7. When the pastry is golden and crisp, remove from the oven and slit down one side to release the steam. (If this is not done, the centre will be soggy.)
8. Switch the oven off and return the choux pastry to the oven in order to dry out the centres for 15 minutes.
9. It is better to use the choux pastry on the same day. Fill the centres with sweetened whipped cream or cold confectioner's custard, and decorate the top with caramel, chocolate glacé icing or sifted icing sugar.

Confectioner's Custard Filling

This recipe makes 625 ml (2½ cups) filling.

INGREDIENTS

500 ml (16 fl oz, 2 cups) milk
125 ml (120 g, 4 oz, ½ cup) sugar
½ vanilla pod, scraped out, or 5 ml (1 tsp) vanilla essence
4 egg yolks
80 ml (40 g, 1½ oz, 6 tbsp) cornflour

METHOD

1. Heat milk, half the sugar and the vanilla pod (if using).
2. In another bowl, whisk yolks with remaining sugar until creamy. Add vanilla essence if you haven't used a pod.
3. Mix the cornflour with a little milk to form a paste, then add the paste to the egg mixture.
4. Remove vanilla pod (if using) from heated milk mixture and stir milk mixture into egg mixture. Return mixture to the saucepan and the saucepan to the stove.
5. Stir continuously over a gentle heat until the custard coats the back of the wooden spoon.
6. Remove the custard from the heat and strain it through a sieve into a bowl. Cover with plastic wrap and place the custard in the refrigerator when cool. Use it as a filling when it is cold and has thickened.

Ice-cream Cakes

This is an excellent idea for a birthday cake, as very few children will refuse ice-cream. It makes a refreshing alternative to traditional cake, often at a time when children need to cool down after running around and playing rowdy games. After singing 'Happy Birthday', ice-cream can quickly be scooped into cones, or slices can be cut and placed on small paper plates. However, before deciding to make an ice-cream cake, you must ensure that you have sufficient room in your freezer and that your freezer is reliable.

METHOD

1. Choose a cool place near the freezer in which to work. Work quickly when working with ice-cream, and return it to the freezer at the first sign of melting. Where possible, use cake tin moulds to achieve the desired shape. Have a cake board ready. Spoon the softened ice-cream directly into the tin and place it in the freezer to firm. Once firm, remove the ice-cream mould from the freezer and invert it onto the cake board on which it is to be served. Cover the tin with a hot cloth to release the ice-cream shape onto the board, then re-freeze immediately.
2. If you wish to do free moulding (i.e. not making use of a mould), choose the shape of the cake you would like and mould the ice-cream straight onto the cake board. Free moulding is made easier if you have an ornament or toy to copy. You could, for example, use a Dalmatian rubber toy if you are thinking of making the Dalmatian ice-cream puppy. It may be necessary to place the ice-cream in the freezer during the moulding process, especially if the edges start to melt.
3. Using a palette knife and a spoon, mould all the thick areas first, leaving the small, thin parts till last.
4. Once the design is complete and three-dimensional moulding is achieved, the ice-cream shape must be left overnight in the freezer to become really firm.
5. Set out all the decorating ingredients and equipment (sweets, coloured whipped cream, butter icing, piping bags, etc.) where you will be working, so that everything is on hand and ready for you to use.
6. To cover large areas, use sweetened whipped cream, butter icing, piping jelly or paintwork.
7. When doing paintwork on the ice-cream cake, use water to mix the food colouring. Dip the paintbrush in water if it sticks to the ice-cream. Do not use too much water on the surface of the cake as it will form ice, which will blur the paintwork.
8. Lastly, finish off with the detailed areas, such as the facial features and accessories. Make sure you use sweets of which the colour will not run on the ice cream. Pipe the writing on the cake using coloured whipped cream, piping jelly, melted chocolate or butter icing. Place the candles on the cake and then freeze it until ready to serve.
9. After serving, remember to return the remaining ice-cream cake to the freezer. Do not leave the cake on the table as you would do with most birthday cakes.

NOTE

Sweetened whipped cream lasts longer on ice-cream than butter icing and is not as rich. However, if you use butter icing, colours will appear brighter.

Fondant Icing

Other names for fondant icing are sugarpaste or plastic icing. It is easy to make and use, gives a professional finish to any cake, and can be bought from most supermarkets and cake icing shops. This recipe makes 1 kg (2 lb) icing, enough to cover one deep 18 cm (7 in) cake.

INGREDIENTS

30 ml (15 g, ½ oz, 2 tbsp) gelatine
60 ml (2 fl oz, ¼ cup) cold water
30 ml (1 fl oz, 2 tbsp) glycerine
125 ml (4 fl oz, ½ cup) liquid glucose
750 g (1 lb 8 oz, 6 cups) icing sugar, sifted
2 ml (½ tsp) rose water
Food colouring
60 ml (25 g, 1 oz, 4 tbsp) cornflour, sifted together with the same amount of icing sugar

METHOD

1. In a heatproof bowl, mix the gelatine and the cold water, then dissolve over hot water, stirring all the time. Leave to cool slightly.
2. Add the glycerine and liquid glucose.
3. Pour the gelatine mixture into a big bowl and gradually add icing sugar, mixing well until it becomes dough-like.
4. Add rose water and then add food colouring drop by drop until the desired depth of colour is achieved.
5. Knead on a surface sprinkled with the cornflour and icing sugar, until it has the consistency of plasticine.
6. Using a large rolling pin, roll out the mixture evenly on the sifted cornflour and icing sugar surface, keeping the surface smooth and large enough to cover the top and sides of the cake.
7. If you are icing a fruit cake, you would cover it with apricot glaze and marzipan, then brush it with beaten egg white and cover with fondant icing. Use a rolling pin to lift and place the fondant icing centrally over the cake. Madeira and oil sponge cakes can be brushed with apricot glaze or spread with butter icing before covering with the fondant icing.
8. In order to achieve a perfectly even surface and sides, it is a good idea to dust your hands with icing sugar before smoothing the fondant icing over the cake in circular movements. Pierce any air bubbles with a pin. Cut away excess icing at the base.

NOTE

The cake iced with fondant icing is best left for at least a day before doing any decorative icing on the cake, with the exception of inlaid work, which should be done straight away, before the fondant icing dries and firms.

Royal Icing

This produces a hard, brittle but satin-like finish when used as icing. The recipe makes 200 g (7 oz, ⅔ cup) icing.

INGREDIENTS

1 egg white

400 ml (260 g, 8 oz, 1½ cups) icing sugar, sifted

METHOD

1. Place the egg white in a clean, dry bowl and whisk lightly, using a fork.
2. Gradually add the sifted icing sugar to the whisked egg white, about 25 ml (2 tbsp) at a time, using either a wooden spoon or an electric mixer to produce a smooth, white, shiny icing.
3. Adjust the consistency by adding more or less icing sugar, depending on what the icing is to be used for (you need a firmer texture for piping borders and a softer consistency for writing or line work).
4. Keep excess icing in a bowl covered with plastic or a damp cloth to prevent hardening. Also keep the ends of tubes filled with royal icing airtight to prevent hardening and subsequent blocking of the tube.
5. Royal icing will keep for up to three days in an airtight container that is stored in the refrigerator. Stir the icing well before using it.

Butter Icing

Butter icing is a versatile, rich, creamy icing that is easy to make and work with and which children probably enjoy the most. It can be swirled or piped, and forms a delicious filling and coating for sponge, swiss roll and Madeira cakes. This recipe makes 500 g (1 lb) icing, which is enough for a 20 cm (8 in) cake.

INGREDIENTS

125 g (4 oz) butter or margarine

750 ml (480 g, 15 oz, 3 cups) icing sugar, sifted

5 ml (1 tsp) flavouring or
45 ml (3 tbsp) cocoa powder

30 ml (1 fl oz, 2 tbsp) milk, water or fruit juice

METHOD

1. Place the butter in a bowl and, using either a wooden spoon or an electric mixer, beat well until soft.
2. Gradually add the sifted icing sugar, beating the mixture well after each addition, until the icing becomes light and fluffy. (If making chocolate icing, add cocoa powder to the icing sugar before sifting.)
3. Add flavouring (if using), then the liquid (milk, water or juice) to achieve a smooth spreading consistency.
4. Preferably use a metal palette knife to spread the icing smoothly over the cake.
5. Butter icing will keep for up to five days if stored in an airtight container in the refrigerator.

Apricot Glaze

Apricot glaze is used for brushing on Madeira, oil sponge or fruit cakes before applying marzipan or fondant icing.

INGREDIENTS
250 ml (250 g, 8 oz, 1 cup) smooth apricot jam
30 ml (2 tbsp) water

METHOD
1. Put the jam and the water into a saucepan, bring to the boil and simmer gently for approximately one minute. Alternatively, put both the ingredients into a glass bowl, mix together, cover with plastic wrap and microwave on medium for about one minute.
2. Brush the apricot jam mixture smoothly and evenly over the surface of the cake while the glaze is still hot. This will seal the cake and act as an adhering agent for the marzipan or fondant icing.

Seven-minute Frosting

This is a light, meringue-like icing that crisps on the outside when it is left to dry. The frosting can be decorated with sweets before it dries, but decorating with fruit must be done on the dried, crisp frosting just before serving, as the enzymes in fresh fruit cause the frosting to dissolve slightly.

INGREDIENTS
2 egg whites
60 ml (2 fl oz, ¼ cup) water
45 ml (3 tbsp) golden syrup
10 ml (2 tsp) cream of tartar
500 ml (320 g, 10 oz, 2 cups) icing sugar, sifted

METHOD
1. Place the egg whites, water, golden syrup and cream of tartar in a heatproof bowl or the top of a double boiler and whisk the mixture with an electric mixer until it is thoroughly blended.
2. Stir in the sifted icing sugar and then place the bowl containing the mixture over a saucepan of simmering water (or use a double boiler) and whisk the mixture until it becomes thick and white. The simmering water should not touch the base of the bowl.
3. Remove the bowl from the saucepan using protective gloves, then continue to whisk the frosting until it is completely cool, thick and smooth and the mixture stands up in soft peaks.
4. Use the frosting immediately to fill and cover the cakes. It can be spread smoothly or swirled and peaked into a soft coating, using a palette knife.

CHOUX PASTRY

Beehive

EQUIPMENT

1 piping bag
Plastic bee moulds
2 substitute piping bags (see page 75)
36 cm (14 in) round cake board
Heavy-based frying pan

INGREDIENTS

300 g (11 oz) caramel chocolate, for the bees
50 g (1¾ oz) white chocolate, for decorating the bees
50 g (1¾ oz) dark chocolate, for decorating the bees
2 x Choux Pastry recipe (see page 9)
500 ml (16 fl oz, 2 cups) Confectioner's Custard (see page 9)
250 ml (200 g, 1 cup) granulated white sugar
Egg white
Brown sugar for the cake board

1. First make 35–40 chocolate bees. Melt the caramel chocolate (see page 81) and, when completely smooth, place in the piping bag. Snip off the tip and pipe melted chocolate into the plastic bee moulds.
2. When the chocolate sets, remove the bees from the moulds. Using substitute piping bags, decorate bees with melted white chocolate for the wings and melted dark chocolate stripes for the bodies. Each type of chocolate must have its own piping bag, the tip of which is removed just prior to piping. The amount snipped off each bag depends on the thickness of the piping required. Store the bees in a sealed container.
3. Make 36 choux and when completely cool, fill them with confectioner's custard. Arrange 12 of the choux on the cake board.
4. Place the white sugar in the frying pan and slowly caramelize, stirring with a wooden spoon until the syrup that forms is clear and lightly golden. Immediately remove caramel from the stove before it burns, and drizzle a little over the first layer of choux on the board. Working quickly, build up subsequent layers of choux with drizzled caramel to form a hive.
5. While the caramel is still warm, attach the chocolate bees to the entire surface of the hive.
6. Brush the cake board with egg white (so that the sugar will stick to the board) and sprinkle brown sugar around the hive and into the entrance (see photograph).
7. Assemble the beehive about 2–3 hours before serving to prevent the caramel topping from dissolving.

HANDY HINTS

1. When cleaning the frying pan, the caramel left in the pan must be allowed to cool down before any water is poured into the pan. Leave the water in the pan for several hours. The caramel will soon dissolve into the water, making the pan easier to clean.
2. Be very careful when working with hot caramel as it can cause severe burns.

Bird of Paradise

EQUIPMENT

46 cm (18 in) oval cake board
Knitting needle
Template (see page 84)
Palette knife and spoon
4 substitute piping bags (see page 75)
1 piping bag
Number 5 star tube

INGREDIENTS

3 litres (5 pints) vanilla ice-cream
Yellow, red and green piping jelly (see page 78)
100 g (3 oz) dark chocolate, melted
Yellow Jelly Tot (for the eye)
1–2 Flake chocolate bars (for the bird's perch)
25 g (1 oz, 2 tbsp) yellow butter icing or 3 yellow liquorice comforts (for the claws)

1. Using the template, trace the outline of the bird lightly onto the cake board with the knitting needle, without damaging the surface of the cake board.
2. Spoon the vanilla ice-cream directly onto the cake board within the outlined area. Working quickly, mould the ice-cream into the shape of a bird using a palette knife and a spoon (see page 10). Re-freeze until the ice-cream is completely firm.
3. Fill each of three substitute piping bags with one of the three piping jellies.
4. Melt the chocolate and pour it into the piping bag without removing the tip of the bag.
5. Remove the frozen ice-cream bird from the freezer. Using a skewer, score the top surface of the bird, dividing it into separate areas for the different colours. Snip off the tip of the chocolate piping bag and pipe lines along these demarcated lines (see photograph). Pipe a small chocolate dot (pupil) on the yellow Jelly Tot (the bird's eye).
6. Snip the tips off the substitute bags of jelly and pipe the colours onto the different demarcated areas, completely filling the outlined spaces.
7. Position the yellow Jelly Tot (the bird's eye) on the head and attach the Flake chocolate bar (the branch) under the bird's body. Lastly, pipe the bird's elongated claws using a star tube, yellow icing and a substitute piping bag, or use yellow liquorice comforts.
8. Re-freeze until ready for serving.

HANDY HINT

Ensure that the demarcated areas where the jelly is to be piped are flat, not sloping, otherwise the jelly will slide off due to its slippery nature.

Kite

EQUIPMENT

40 cm (16 in) oval cake board
Palette knife
3 piping bags
6 mm (¼ in) large star tube
2 x 10 mm (⅜ in) large plain tubes

INGREDIENTS

3 litres (5 pints) vanilla ice cream
150 g (5 oz) vanilla Butter Icing (see page 12)
500 g (1 lb) Butter Icing (see page 12)
Green food colouring
Pink and orange Jelly Tots (to decorate the kite)
One pink, two orange, one green Fizz bar (for bows)
Three grape candy straws (for kite string and mouth)
Two orange seeded Liquorice All-sorts (for buttons)
Three flying saucer sherbet sweets (for eyes and nose)
Two black Jelly Tots (for eyes)

1. Spoon vanilla ice-cream onto the cake board and, using a palette knife, mould into the kite shape. Freeze until completely firm.
2. Prepare the vanilla butter icing. Colour the 500 g (1 lb) butter icing with the green food colouring. Set aside some of the green icing for decorating the sides of the kite.
3. Divide the remaining green icing in half, placing half in the piping bag with the star tube and the other half in a piping bag with a plain tube. Place the vanilla icing in the remaining piping bag with the plain tube.
4. Prepare the sweets for decoration and twist the Fizz bars to make bows (see page 82).
5. Using a skewer, score the top surface of the kite, dividing it into demarcated areas (see photograph).
6. Using a palette knife, spread the green butter icing on the sides of the cake.
7. Pipe one section of the kite with green icing and the section diagonally opposite with vanilla icing, using long lines (see photograph).
8. Fill in the remaining two sections using Jelly Tots.
9. Re-freeze, if necessary, before completing the facial features of the kite using sweets.
10. Using a star tube, decorate the base and top edge of the kite with green butter icing.
11. Decorate the cake board with grape candy straws interspersed with twisted Fizz bar bows. Re-freeze until ready to serve.

HANDY HINT

When doing piped work on ice-cream, you can always substitute the butter icing with whipped cream coloured with food colouring (see page 10).

Dalmatian Pup

EQUIPMENT

35 cm (14 in) round cake tin
46 cm (18 in) round cake board
Sharp knife
23 cm (9 in) round cake board
2 piping bags
Number 3 writing tube
Basket weave tube
Palette knife or modelling tool (see page 75)

INGREDIENTS

2 x Oil Sponge Cake recipe, using 8 eggs, for the basket (see page 7)
1½ kg (3 lb) chocolate Butter Icing (see page 12)
4 litres (6½ pints) vanilla ice-cream
1 Flake chocolate bar
100 g (3½ oz) dark chocolate, melted (for the Dalmatian pup's spots)
3 liquorice sweets (for the nose and eyeballs)
1 liquorice strip (for the eyebrows, claws and rings around the eyes)
1 pink marshmallow (for the tongue)
Blue sour candy belt (for the collar)
Dalmatian candles

1. Make a large round oil sponge cake, place it on the larger cake board and cut a ring out of the centre using a sharp knife and a round template, 25 cm (10 in) in diameter.
2. Remove this central cake and freeze it to use on another occasion.
3. Cut away a small section, about 13 cm (5 in) long and half the height of the finished cake, to represent the basket's entrance (see photograph).
4. Spread a thin layer of chocolate butter icing over the sponge cake basket.
5. Commence the basket work on the sponge cake basket (see page 77 for the basket weave technique). Start from the centre back of the basket cake and, working round to the front, spiral the basket weave as you progress.
6. To make the ice-cream Dalmatian pup, spoon the ice-cream onto the smaller cake board and mould into a pup shape using an ornament or child's toy as a reference (see page 10).
7. Insert the Flake chocolate bar through the neck of the pup to strengthen it before modelling the head. The height of the completed pup should be approximately 20 cm (8 in).
8. Re-freeze the pup whenever the first signs of melting are evident.
9. Use a small palette knife or a modelling tool (see page 75) to mould the small facial features (such as the mouth cavity, ears, etc.) and the paws.
10. Create the Dalmatian's spots by spooning melted chocolate onto non-stick baking paper in small rounds of irregular shape and size.
11. Remove the ice-cream pup from the freezer and place the chocolate spots in position over the body, then place the liquorice sweets and cut liqourice strips onto the pup's face (see photograph).
12. Cut a slice off a pink marshmallow and place in the mouth cavity to represent a tongue. Lastly, drape the blue sour candy belt (for the collar) around the pup's neck and place it back in the freezer.

13. Remove the ice-cream Dalmatian pup from the freezer just before serving and gently lower it (complete with its small cake board) into the space allowed in the cake basket. Decorate the top edge of the pup's basket with the Dalmatian candles.

HANDY HINT

The Dalmatian pup is most versatile, as it gives children a choice of either a piece of cake from the basket or some 'spotted' ice-cream.

Galleon

EQUIPMENT

46 cm (18 in) oval cake board
Knitting needle
Palette knife
Sharp knife
1 piping bag
7 mm (¼ in) star tube
30 cm (12 in) x wooden skewer or dowel stick, 2 mm (⅛ in) in diameter

INGREDIENTS

4 litres (6½ pints) chocolate ice-cream
1 kg (2 lb) chocolate Butter Icing (see page 12) or 600 ml (1 pint) whipped cream, sweetened and flavoured with chocolate
Chocolate Matchmakers or Choc Stix (for the bow decoration and the oars)
Rice paper
Red and black food colouring (for flags)
Candy bars (for the masts)
250 ml (8 fl oz, 1 cup) whipped cream
Blue and green food colouring (for the sea)
Jelly Tots (for sides of galleon)
Chocolate Holey Moleys (for the portholes)
Pirate candles

1. Lightly draw the shape of the base of the galleon directly onto the cake board, using a knitting needle. Spoon mounds of the chocolate ice-cream into the outline on the board and then mould into the shape of the galleon using a palette knife (see photograph).
2. Return the ice-cream galleon to the freezer when it shows signs of melting. Take the galleon out only when it is firm again.
3. Smooth the sides of the ice-cream galleon with the palette knife and then create the tiered effect by cutting sections of the decks away with a sharp knife (see photograph). Return to the freezer.
4. Prepare the piping bag with the star tube and fill it with either chocolate butter icing or sweetened chocolate whipped cream.
5. Working quickly, pipe the sides of the galleon and then place two Matchmakers in the front bow position. Return galleon to the freezer.
6. Cut four sails measuring 12 x 8 cm (5 x 3 in) from the rice paper. Cut flags and paint with food colouring: two red and two with the skull and crossbone symbol.
7. Lace the candy bars and the central skewer through the sails and then attach the rice paper flags.
8. Whip the cream for the sea, then add the blue and green food colouring, mixing it only slightly in order to achieve an uneven effect. Remove the galleon from the freezer and attach the sweets and the sails, and then spread the coloured whipped cream on the cake board around the galleon to represent the sea. Insert the chocolate Matchmaker oars into the chocolate Holey Moley portholes. Place the candles in position on the deck.

HANDY HINT

Do not be tempted to work too long on the ice-cream galleon, especially once the butter icing has been piped on, because the icing will fall off in sections if the ice-cream begins to melt. If the ice-cream base is not completely firm, it is preferable to pipe with chocolate whipped cream, which adheres to the ice-cream better than butter icing does.

Ice-cream Horse

EQUIPMENT

Template (see page 83)
50 cm (20 in) square cake board
Palette knife and spoon
3 paintbrushes (fine, medium, large)
Plastic riding cap mould
Metal skewer
1 piping bag
5 mm (¼ in) large star tube

INGREDIENTS

6 litres (10 pints) vanilla ice-cream
Food colouring (black, brown, yellow and orange)
200 g (7 oz) dark chocolate, melted (for riding caps)
250 ml (8 fl oz, 1 cup) whipped cream
Gold candles

1. Using the template, trace the outline of the horse and horseshoe onto the board. Spoon ice-cream onto the horse shape and mould the head and neck with a palette knife and spoon (see page 10). Re-freeze frequently during moulding. (Moulding is made much easier when copying an ornamental or toy horse.)
2. Prepare the food colouring (see page 79) by mixing the colours required and only then remove the moulded ice-cream from the freezer for painting. Working quickly, apply the food colouring to the ice-cream horse, beginning with the lighter shades and ending with the darker (see photograph). Re-freeze during painting as many times as you find necessary.
3. Remove the painted horse from the freezer and spoon more ice-cream around the horse's head in the shape of a horseshoe, following the tracing of the template.
4. Smooth the horseshoe with a palette knife. Put the ice-cream horse back into the freezer.
5. Make eight chocolate riding caps using the plastic mould (see page 10) or buy ready-made chocolate riding caps for convenience.
6. Fill the piping bag with whipped cream and pipe stars around the horseshoe to neaten the edges.
7. Pierce the chocolate riding caps with a hot skewer and insert the gold candles. Arrange them around the horseshoe.

HANDY HINT

Do not use much water when mixing food colouring powder or paste (see page 79) as it can form a layer of ice over the painted area and blur the paintwork.

Fruit Butterfly

EQUIPMENT

23 cm (9 in) square cake tin
Sharp knife
46 cm (18 in) square cake board
Palette knife
Metal skewer

INGREDIENTS

1 x Oil Sponge Cake recipe, using 4 eggs (see page 7)
2 mini swiss rolls (for the body of the butterfly)
Seven-minute Frosting, using 3 egg whites (see page 13)
4 chocolate Sweetie Pies (which can also be used as candle holders)
Any fresh fruit in season, such as strawberries, kiwi fruit, bananas, cling peaches, grapes and cherries (use cherries with their stalks on as feelers)
Candles

1. Using a square tin, make the oil sponge cake.
2. Leave the cake to cool completely, and then use a sharp knife to cut it diagonally in half to form the two wings of the butterfly (see illustration).
3. Cut off two 5 cm (2 in) triangles from the two opposite right-angled edges of the cake (see illustration).
4. Position the mini swiss rolls on the cake board.
5. Place the wings on the cake board so that the parts where the triangles have been removed face in towards the body of the butterfly.

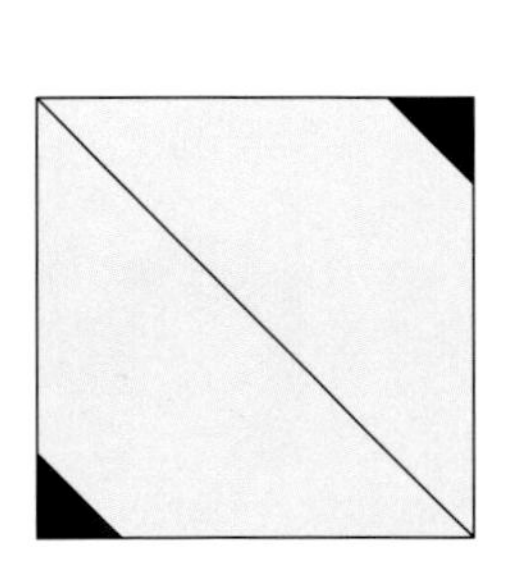

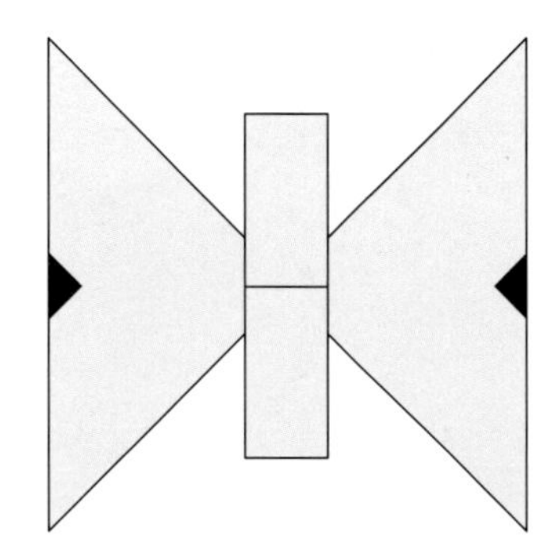

6. Cut two more 5 cm (2 in) triangles from the outer edges of the wings so that the butterfly looks as if it has four wings instead of two (see illustration).
7. Make the frosting and, using a palette knife, immediately spread it over the entire cake.
8. Cover the cake well, even at the base, to seal it so as to keep it fresh.
9. Place the chocolate Sweetie Pies in position as shown on the photograph.
10. Allow the frosting to set in the refrigerator or in a cool place before decorating the cake with fruit.
11. Wash and prepare the fruit. Slice neatly and place on a covered tray, ready for use. If you use bananas, remember to squeeze lemon juice over them to prevent them from browning.
12. Decorate the butterfly with the prepared fruit an hour before serving.
13. Pierce the Sweetie Pies by heating the tip of a metal skewer or knitting needle in boiling water, and insert the candles in the holes.

Royal Crown

EQUIPMENT

15 cm (6 in) deep round cake tin
23 cm (9 in) round cake board
Palette knife
1 piping bag
Number 7 star tube

INGREDIENTS

½–¾ x Madeira Cake recipe, using 2–3 eggs (see page 6)
200 g (7 oz) Butter Icing (see page 12) or Fondant Icing (see page 11) coloured with red food colouring powder, or ready-made red fondant
14 large wafer biscuits (for the crown)
500 g (1 lb) vanilla Butter Icing (see page 12)
Gold sugar-coated almonds (for the jewels)
Gold balls (for the gold nuggets)
25 white marshmallows (for the ermine or fur on the crown)
Black, yellow and green Jelly Tots (for the jewels)
7 red fruit sparkles (for the jewels)
7 black fruit sparkles (for the jewels)

1. Pour the Madeira cake mixture into the cake tin, deliberately peaking the mixture in the centre prior to baking to ensure that the baked cake is domed.
2. Allow the cake to cool completely and then centre it on the cake board.
3. Colour the icing with red food colouring powder and spread over the cake, smoothing it with a heated palette knife. Alternatively, brush the cake with Apricot Glaze (see page 13) and then cover it with ready-made red fondant icing.
4. Lay two wafer biscuits together for each section of the crown and cut away the two top edges of the biscuits equally, forming a point (see illustration). Repeat for all the crown sections.

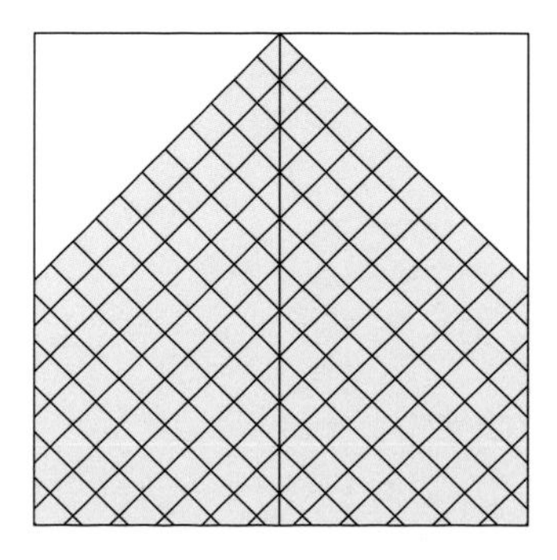

5. Spread wafer sections (front and back) with vanilla butter icing and attach to the sides of the cake, resting the base of the wafer on the cake board.
6. Using a hot palette knife, smooth the icing on the inside and the outside of the wafers.
7. Pipe stars along the top edge of the crown, using vanilla butter icing and the star tube.
8. Decorate the tips of the crown with gold sugar-coated almonds and place gold balls along the piped edge.
9. Line the base of the crown with halved marshmallows. Dot with black Jelly Tots at regular intervals.
10. Decorate the sides (see photograph) by attaching the rest of the Jelly Tots, the red and black fruit sparkles and gold sugar-coated almonds to the butter icing.

HANDY HINT

Place the marshmallows cut side down to prevent them slipping off the board.

Clown

EQUIPMENT

23 cm (9 in) round cake tin
40 cm (16 in) round cake board
Palette knife
1 piping bag
5 mm (¼ in) large star tube

INGREDIENTS

½ x Oil Sponge Cake recipe, using 2 eggs (see page 7)
500 g (1 lb) vanilla Butter Icing (see page 12)
Yellow and pink food colouring
Red lollipop (for the nose)
2 yellow round sweets (for the cheeks)
Dots of black liquorice (for the eyes)
Red and green sour candy straws (for outlining the eyes, mouth and hat band)
1 blue, 1 yellow and 1 red sour candy belt (cut and shaped for the eyeballs, eyelids, eyebrows and mouth)
Strawberry twizzlers (for the hair)
Emerald food colouring
Oval sweet (badge for the hat)
17 tangerine (orange) Fizz bars
21 strawberry (pink) Fizz bars
20 cream soda (green) Fizz bars
Clown candles

HANDY HINTS

1. Fizz bars cannot be prepared too early as they will not hold the rounded shape required.
2. Always buy more Fizz bars than you need in case of breakage.

1. Bake the round oil sponge cake then leave to cool completely. Centre it on the round cake board.
2. Add drops of the yellow and pink food colouring to half of the butter icing to achieve the flesh colour.
3. Spread 90 g (3 oz) of the white vanilla icing over the mouth and eye areas.
4. Spread flesh-coloured butter icing evenly over the remainder of the cake. Smooth the icing using a palette knife dipped in boiling water.
5. When the icing has set, decorate the clown's face with the sweets (see photograph).
6. Place the twizzler hair in position.
7. Colour the remaining white icing with emerald food colouring and, using the 5 mm (¼ in) star tube, pipe on the hat.
8. Decorate the hat with a sour candy straw hat band and the oval sweet.
9. Just before serving, gently fold the Fizz bars in half (see page 82) and place them around the base of the cake to form the collar.
10. To complete the arrangement, place the clown candles on the cake board.

Teddy Bear's Picnic

EQUIPMENT

Teddy bear cake tin
Wooden board
Substitute piping bag (see page 75)
Fork
Crimper, modelling tool or tweezers
Paintbrushes (fine or medium)
Food colouring pen (colour of your choice)

INGREDIENTS

¾ x Oil Sponge Cake recipe, using 3 eggs (see page 7)
1 kg (2 lb) Butter Icing (see page 12)
Yellow food colouring
50 ml (25 g, 1 oz, 4 tbsp) cocoa powder, sifted
Liquorice strips (for the mouth)
Liquorice sweets (for the nose and pupils of the eye)
Chocolate buttons (for the eyes)
Chocolate balls (for the paws)
50 g (1¾ oz) Fondant Icing (see page 11)
Food colouring (colour of your choice)
White chocolate buttons (for picnic treats)
3 small white sweets (for picnic treats)
Teddy bear candles

1. Make the teddy bear-shaped oil sponge cake and allow it to cool completely before icing.
2. Centre the cake on the wooden board.
3. Mix three-quarters of the butter icing with yellow food colouring and three-quarters of the sifted cocoa powder to form a caramel brown colour.
4. Mix the remaining quarter of the icing to a pale brown colour (use the remaining cocoa powder and a little yellow food colouring to achieve the desired colour).
5. Using the photograph as a guide, spread the dark caramel icing over the teddy bear cake, excluding the four paw pads, the ears and the nose area. Spread the pale brown icing over the smaller areas.
6. Add a little more cocoa powder to the remaining icing mixture and place icing in a substitute piping bag.
7. Snip the tip off the piping bag and pipe the icing around the teddy's ears.
8. Roughen the icing on the teddy's body with a fork to give the effect of fur.
9. Place the teddy bear's mouth (liquorice strip) and its nose (the liquorice sweet) in position. For the teddy bear's eyes, use the chocolate buttons topped with liquorice pupils.
10. Finish off the teddy bear's paws with the chocolate buttons or chocolate balls.
11. Make the blanket by rolling out the fondant icing into a square (see page 80). Frill the edges using a crimper, a modelling tool or even a pair of tweezers. Paint the edges of the blanket with food colouring of your choice. Paint 'Happy Birthday' on the blanket, or write it using a food colouring pen.
12. Drape the blanket over the centre of the teddy bear. Arrange the sweetie picnic treats and teddy candles on the blanket (see photograph).

Happy
Birthday

Aquarium or Dolphinarium

EQUIPMENT

23 cm (9 in) deep cake tin or 2 x 23 cm round cake tins
30 cm (12 in) round cake board
1 piping bag
7 mm (⅓ in) large star tube
Pastry brush
Clear plastic florist's stick
Clear fishing line

INGREDIENTS

1¼ x Oil Sponge Cake recipe, using 5 eggs (see page 7)
750 g (1½ lb) Butter Icing (see page 12)
Blue food colouring
9 blue sour candy straws (for the window frames and the jelly dolphin ring support)
8 crystallized jelly rings (4 for lifebelts on walls of tank and 4 as rings for the dolphin tricks)
Fish, dolphins and turtles (jelly sweets or gums)
125 ml (125 g, ½ cup) clear piping jelly (see page 78)
White Liquorice All-sorts (for the coping around the tank)
1 large lollipop (for supporting the rod with the jelly rings)
Seaworld candle

1. Make the round oil sponge cake or cakes and leave to cool completely.
2. Make the butter icing and add enough blue food colouring to make it pale blue.
3. Centre the cake or cakes on the cake board and cover completely with the pale blue butter icing.
4. Create the four windows of the aquarium or dolphinarium by cutting the blue candy straws to form frames.
5. Decorate the sides of the cake, using a piping bag fitted with a star tube and the remaining blue butter icing. Pipe straight vertical lines of blue icing around the sides of the cake.
6. Neaten the top and bottom edge of the cake with a row of piped stars.
7. Place the jelly rings (lifebelts) at equal distances between the aquarium windows.
8. Fill the windows with fish and turtles. Add blue food colouring to the clear piping jelly and, using a pastry brush, brush the window areas lightly with the blue jelly (see page 78).
9. Brush the top of the cake with blue jelly.
10. Place the Liquorice All-sorts around the top edge of the cake to represent coping tiles.
11. Place the lollipop stick firmly into one side of the cake and drape the blue candy straw over it, supporting the candy straw on the other side with the clear florist's stick. Thread four jelly rings onto the blue candy straw.
12. Place the dolphins, the fish and the seaworld candle on the jelly surface.
13. Suspend the dolphin from the candy straw using clear fishing line threaded through the dolphin's nose.

HANDY HINT

Remember to remove and discard the fishing line before the jumping dolphin is eaten.

HAPPY
BIRTHDAY

Children's Playground

EQUIPMENT

7.5 cm (3 in) insulated round plate (for the carousel)
Carousel candles
33 x 23 x 5 cm (13 x 9 x 2 in) rectangular cake tin
50 x 30 cm (20 x 12 in) rectangular cake board
Serrated icing comb (see page 75)
Plastic fence

INGREDIENTS

Chocolate Matchmakers
100 g (3½ oz) dark chocolate, melted
Sour candy belts (pink, blue, yellow and green)
3 large rice cakes
100 g (3½ oz) white chocolate, melted
Spiral rainbow candy lollipop
Pink Jelly Tots
2 chocolate Holey Moleys
1 small rice cake
12 cigarette sweets
1 x Oil Sponge Cake recipe, using 4 eggs (see page 7)
500 g (1 lb) Butter Icing (see page 12)
Green food colouring
Jellybeans (for border around cake)
Ice-cream cone chocolate sweets
Brown sugar (for the sandpit)
Liquorice comforts (for the border of the sandpit)

1. Make the playground equipment of your choice before starting the cake, and set aside in a safe place.
2. To make the jungle gym, trim the chocolate Matchmakers and, using melted chocolate, combine to make a four-sided jungle gym. Attach the candy belt slide using melted chocolate.
3. To make the carousel, sandwich two of the rice cakes together with the melted white chocolate and cover the sides with pink candy belts. Pierce the rice cakes with the sharpened stick of the rainbow lollipop.
4. Make the carousel roof cover. If the candles are to be lit in the carousel, make the carousel roof by attaching the remaining rice cake to the insulated round plate. Cover the rice cake with melted white chocolate and finish with strips of sour candy belts radiating from the centre.
5. Decorate the sides with Jelly Tots and stick the carousel roof on top of the rainbow lollipop using melted chocolate. Place the carousel candles on the rice cake platform.
6. To make the swings, trim the Matchmakers and then join them together with melted chocolate to form a support for the swings. Attach a Holey Moley to a Matchmaker (centre rope) to form each of the swings.
7. To make the roundabout, cover the small rice cake in melted white chocolate, using a pastry brush, and then attach the candy belt strip around the side. Place the white cigarette sweets radially in position, securing them with melted white chocolate. Place a pink Jelly Tot in the centre.
8. Now make the rectangular oil sponge cake. When it is completely cool, centre the cake on the cake board.

9. Colour the butter icing with the green food colouring and spread the green icing smoothly over the top and around the sides of the cake. Decorate the sides of the cake using the serrated icing comb.
10. To decorate the playground cake, place the jelly beans around the base of the cake and then arrange the ice-cream cone sweets around the sides of the cake. Arrange the playground equipment on top of the cake. Make the sandpit using the brown sugar bordered with the liquorice comforts. Finally, place the plastic fence in position along the back edge of the cake.

HANDY HINT

Only light the candles in the carousel if the roof of the carousel is insulated. Otherwise place suitable candles around the playground.

Circus Time

EQUIPMENT

23 cm (9 in) deep hexagonal cake tin
23 cm (9 in) deep square cake tin
50 cm (20 in) round cake board
3 piping bags
2 x 6 mm (¼ in) large star tubes
Number 5 star tube
Plastic circus animals

INGREDIENTS

1¼ x Madeira Cake recipe, using 5 eggs (see page 6)
1¼ x Oil Sponge Cake recipe, using 5 eggs (see page 7)
2 mini swiss rolls (for portico entrance to tent)
2 kg (4 lb) vanilla Butter Icing (see page 12)
Yellow food colouring
Jelly Tots (for the coloured lights)
9 large wafer biscuits
6 chocolate finger biscuits (wheel supports)
50 g (1¾ oz) dark chocolate, melted
Chocolate Matchmakers (bars for animal cages)
12 Lifesaver sweets (for the wheels)
Orange Jelly Tots (coloured lights around top of caravan)
Yellow Liquorice All-sorts (windows and chimneys)
Egg white
Green coconut (for the grass)
Brown sugar (for the path)
Large pinwheel lollipop (for aerial decoration)
2 yellow lollipops (to highlight the entrance to the circus arena)
2 yellow and white candy bars (lamps for pathway)
Yellow Jelly Tots
Circus candles

1. Make the Madeira cake and the oil sponge cake, using the hexagonal cake tin and the square cake tin respectively. Allow the cakes to cool completely before you apply any icing.
2. Prepare the board by making 3 holes in the positions where the large lollipop and the two entrance lolli - pops will be placed. The holes must be made before you start icing the cake, to avoid damaging the icing.
3. Place the hexagonal cake (the base of the tent) towards the back of the cake board to allow space in the foreground for the cages and gypsy caravan.
4. Cut the square cake diagonally into quarters. Cut two of the quarters in half. Assemble the tent, placing two large pieces across the middle of the hexagonal cake and small pieces on each side (see illustration). Shave the cake if necessary to create the tent shape.
5. Cut the swiss rolls in half and place them on top of each other against the side of the hexagonal cake to form the portico entrance to the tent.

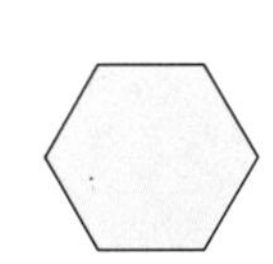
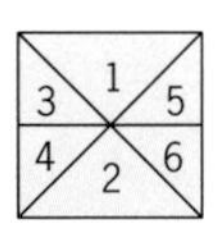

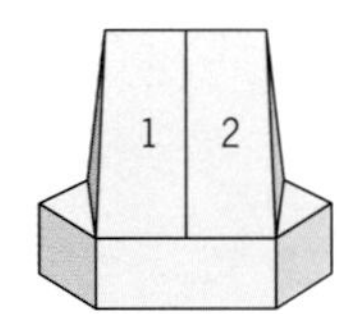

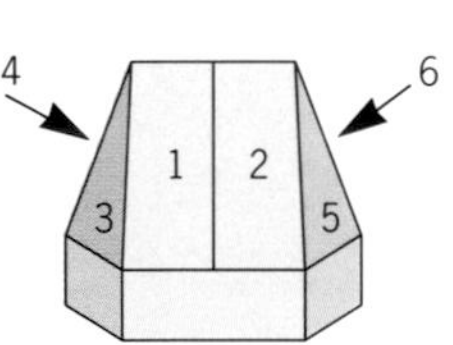

6. Cover tent cake with a third of the vanilla butter icing.
7. Divide the remaining icing in half and colour one half with yellow food colouring.
8. Pipe stars over the tent, using one 6 mm (¼ in) star tube for white icing and the other for yellow icing (see photograph). Using the number 5 star tube and yellow icing, pipe curtains at the entrance to the tent (also use to decorate the cages and caravan).
9. Place the Jelly Tots around the sides of the tent to resemble the coloured lights of a circus tent.
10. To make the bases of the animal cages and the caravan, cut the six finger biscuits to the width of the wafer biscuits. Attach two finger biscuits to the base

of three wafer biscuits in the position of the wheel axles, using the melted chocolate.

11. For the cages, cut the Matchmakers to 6 cm (2½ in) in length. Position the plastic animals on two of the raised wafer biscuit bases and surround with Matchmakers, using melted chocolate and placing them upright around the edge of the wafer.
12. To make the gypsy caravan, use melted chocolate to attach two whole wafer biscuits to the sides of the remaining wafer biscuit base, and halved wafer biscuits to the two ends.
13. Spread the base of the remaining wafer biscuits with melted chocolate and centre them over the top of the cages and caravan (see photograph).
14. Decorate the caravan and the animal cages with the piped yellow butter icing, using the number 5 star tube (see photograph). Lastly, attach the Lifesaver wheels to all three vans, and orange Jelly Tots and yellow Liquorice All-sorts to the caravan. (Remove the yellow fondant from the Liquorice All-sorts and then attach it to the gypsy caravan to represent the windows.)
15. Brush the cake board with egg white and sprinkle it with green coconut and a path of brown sugar.
16. Position the large pinwheel lollipop, the yellow lollipops at the entrance, the candy bars topped with yellow Jelly Tots to represent lights along the path, the circus caravans and the candles.

The Owl and the Pussycat

EQUIPMENT

Plastic owl mould
Plastic pussycat mould
Plastic fish mould (optional)
Paintbrushes (small and medium)
2 substitute piping bags (see page 75)
Template of guitar (see page 83)
Black food colouring pen
30 x 20 cm (12 x 8 in) football or oval cake tin
36 cm (14 in) round cake board
30 cm (12 in) x wooden skewer or dowel stick, 2 mm (⅛ in) in diameter
Palette knife
1 piping bag
Number 6 star tube

INGREDIENTS

750 g (1½ lb) white chocolate, melted
Food colouring powder (brown, red, yellow and black) and non-toxic paint base
Rice paper (for the sail)
Red food colouring paste
1 chocolate Matchmaker (for the guitar)
Dark and white chocolate, melted (for the guitar)
35 g (1½ oz) Fondant Icing (see page 11)
¾ x Oil Sponge or Madeira Cake recipe, using 3 eggs (see page 6 or 7)
2 espresso wafer biscuits (for seat in boat)
350 g (11 oz) Butter Icing (see page 12)
Green, yellow and blue food colouring
250 g (8 oz) vanilla Butter Icing (see page 12)
Jelly or chocolate fish (see page 81)

1. To make the chocolate owl and pussycat, melt 625 g (1¼ lb) of the white chocolate (see page 81) and fill each half of the pussycat and owl moulds. Close the moulds and leave in refrigerator for 5 minutes. Turn the moulds over, leave for another 5 minutes, then turn at 5-minute intervals until no sound of liquid is heard from inside the moulds when gently shaken (25–30 minutes). Remove owl and pussycat from moulds and shade with food powder mixed with non-toxic paint base. Colour 25 g (1 oz) of the melted white chocolate grey with a little black food powder and make chocolate fish in the fish mould. Alternatively, buy jelly or chocolate fish from a sweet shop.
2. Cut the rice paper sail to measure 18 x 15 cm (7 x 6 in) and paint with red food colouring paste (see page 79). Do this very carefully as rice paper tears easily. Leave it to dry flat.
3. Trace the guitar template outline onto the wrong side of non-stick baking paper. Place the Matchmaker in position and pipe the outline using dark chocolate and a substitute piping bag. Flood the centre (see pages 81–82) with white chocolate, using another substitute piping bag. When chocolate has set, paint in the details (such as the strings) using a fine paintbrush and food colouring powder mixed with non-toxic base, or use a black food colouring pen.
4. Mould the honey jar and the pack of money using fondant icing (see page 80), and allow these to dry before painting them with food colouring. Paint or write '£5' on top of the money.
5. Make the oval oil sponge cake or Madeira cake for the boat. When the cake is completely cool, scoop out part of the centre of the cake, leaving a 2.5 cm (1 in) shell. Place wafer biscuits across the centre of the cake to form a seat.
6. Place the boat on the cake board. Melt the remaining 100 g (3½ oz) white chocolate and brush this over the inside of the boat and the seat to ensure a firm anchor for the dowel stick mast, which is inserted into the cake at this stage. Using food colouring powder,

non-toxic paint base and a fine paintbrush, paint lines on the chocolate once it has set, so that the inside of the boat looks like slatted wood.

7. Colour the 350 g (11 oz) butter icing pea green with green and yellow food colouring and spread over the sides of the cake. Smooth with a heated palette knife.
8. Use a skewer to draw lines in the icing across the outside of the boat. Finish off the top edge of the boat with piped stars.
9. Colour the 250 g (8 oz) vanilla icing unevenly with blue and green food colouring and spread this roughly over the cake board to create the effect of the sea. Place the fish in position on the iced cake board.
10. Attach the chocolate guitar to the owl using melted chocolate and place the owl, the pussycat, the honey jar and the pack of money into the boat. Lastly, carefully weave the sail onto the firmly anchored mast (wooden skewer or dowel stick) of the boat.

Soccer Ball

EQUIPMENT

Soccer ball cake tin or round domed cake tin or bowl
36 cm (14 in) hexagonal cake board
Non-stick baking paper
Pencil and pin
Palette knife
Scissors
1 piping bag
Number 2 writing tube
Plastic soccer players and goals

INGREDIENTS

1 x Madeira or Oil Sponge Cake recipe, using 4 eggs (see page 6 or 7)
1 kg (2 lb) vanilla Butter Icing (see page 12)
15 flat liquorice strips
Dark green food colouring powder or paste
Coloured paper flags or liquorice fondant flags
Toothpicks (for the flags)
Soccer ball candles

1. Make the round domed Madeira or oil sponge cake and allow it to cool completely before placing it in the centre of the cake board.
2. Trace the markings off a real soccer ball or marked soccer cake tin and transfer these markings onto the non-stick baking paper.
3. Cover the cake with half of the vanilla butter icing. Smooth the icing using a heated palette knife.
4. Allow the icing to harden overnight and then drape the tracings over the ball and gently mark the lines with pin pricks.
5. Lay the flat liquorice strips together and cut into hexagonal shapes using the scissors and the tracings.
6. Place these liquorice hexagonal shapes on the butter icing in the traced-out areas, together with the liquorice strips that join the hexagonal shapes to each other (see photograph).
7. Place approximately 50 ml (4 tbsp) of the vanilla butter icing in the prepared piping bag fitted with the number 2 writing tube. Colour the remaining butter icing green and use this to decorate the cake board.
8. Place the goals in position on the board and then, using the prepared piping bag, pipe white lines (see page 77) around the board and in front of the goal posts (see photograph).
9. Neaten the base of the cake with strips of liquorice. Position the players, the flags and the soccer ball candles on the soccer field.

HANDY HINT

It is easier to pipe straight lines on a playing field made with royal, butter or fondant icing than a field made using desiccated coconut.

GOAL

Space Shuttle

EQUIPMENT

Two 25 x 37 cm (10 x 14 in) baking sheets
46 cm (18 in) square cake board covered in blue foil
Sharp knife
Template of wings and tail fin (see page 85)
Non-stick baking paper
2 piping bags
2 x number 2 writing tubes

HANDY HINT

When making the wings and the tail fin, complete one wing before commencing with the next, as the spread chocolate sets quickly, sometimes before all the wafer biscuits have been positioned.

INGREDIENTS

2 x Swiss Roll recipe, using 6 eggs (see page 8)
1 Sweetie Pie (for the nose of the shuttle)
Apricot Glaze (see page 13)
400 g (13 oz) white chocolate, melted
Cream coloured wafers (for the wings and tail fin)
1½ kg (3 lb) Fondant Icing (see page 11)
10 flat liquorice strips (to decorate the space shuttle)
50 g (1¾ oz) white Royal Icing (see page 12)
Liquorice All-sorts (for the windows and the fire)
2 dried prune rolls (for the jet engines)
2 white marshmallows (for the jet engines)
Red and blue food colouring (for the flag)
50 g (1¾ oz) Royal Icing, coloured black (see page 12)
White candyfloss (for the smoke)

1. Make the swiss rolls. When cool, place them end to end on the cake board and, using a sharp knife, taper the front roll slightly. Brush a Sweetie Pie with apricot glaze and attach to the front of the cake.
2. Using the template, draw wings and tail fin onto non-stick baking paper. Spread melted white chocolate on the baking paper, following the lines of the template of the one wing, and press the wafers into position vertically, overlapping every join (see illustration).
3. Spread chocolate over the vertical wafers and place a second layer of wafers horizontally, ensuring wafers overlap on every join (see illustration). Spread top layer of wafers with chocolate and leave to set.
4. Repeat the process with the other wing and tail fin.
5. When chocolate has set, lift one wing from the paper and turn it over. Using a sharp knife and sawing vertically, cut according to the template. Repeat for the second wing and the tail fin. Place each wing against a side of the swiss roll and anchor the tail fin into the back of the swiss roll (see photograph).
6. Brush apricot glaze over the entire space shuttle.

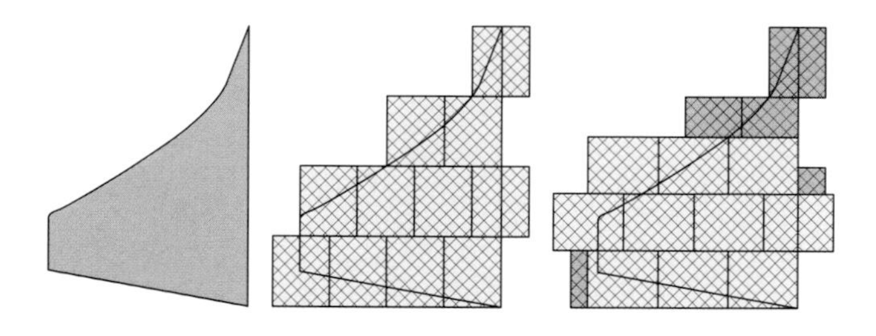

7. Roll out the fondant icing so that it is big enough to cover the shuttle. Lift icing and place over the shuttle, rubbing gently for a smooth surface.
8. Roll a small piece of the remaining fondant icing to form a cone and attach it to the covered Sweetie Pie in the front of the shuttle to form the nose of the shuttle. Cover the join with a strip of flat liquorice.
9. Using royal icing, attach the liquorice across the back wings and surround the outer edge of the entire shuttle with flat liquorice.
10. Create small windows and other details using Liquorice All-sorts and attach them to the shuttle (see photograph). Surround the windows with piped white royal icing (use a number 2 writing tube for this).

11. Cut a prune roll in half and another into four pieces. Using royal icing, attach a round orange Liquorice All-sort (for the fire) to one end of each piece of prune roll. Place the four small jet engines at the rear of the shuttle, topped by a large prune roll on each side of the tail fin. Using royal icing, join the marshmallows to the front ends of the large prune rolls. Paint the American flag on the wing using food colouring.
12. Using black royal icing and a number 2 writing tube, outline tail fin and flag and write 'USA' on other wing.
13. Just before serving, position candyfloss to look as if smoke is flowing out from the back jet engines.

Fire Engine

EQUIPMENT

Plastic bell mould
28 x 10 x 11 cm (11 x 4 x 4½ in) loaf tin
Thin cake board (cut it to fit the base of the loaf tin)
Pastry brush
Sharp knife
50 x 30 cm (20 x 12 in) rectangular cake board
Black food colouring pen
1 substitute piping bag (see page 75)
Number 1 writing tube

INGREDIENTS

Chocolate Matchmakers
50 g (1¾ oz) dark chocolate, melted
50 ml (50 g, 4 tbsp) caster sugar (for the bells)
Gold food colouring powder and non-toxic paint base
1 x Oil Sponge Cake recipe, using 4 eggs (see page 7)
125 ml (4 fl oz, ½ cup) Apricot Glaze (see page 13)
500 g (1 lb) ready-made red fondant icing
25 g (1 oz) white Fondant Icing (see page 11)
Egg white
125 g (4 oz) ready-made black fondant icing
Brown sugar (for the ground)
100 g (3½ oz) green Royal or Butter Icing (see page 12)
Moulded yellow daisies (see page 79)
White cigarette sweets (for the road markings)
3 flat liquorice strips (for the bumpers)
6 liquorice boot laces (for the water hose and tyres)
Yellow Fruit Pastilles (for emergency lights and headlights)
25 g (1 oz) black Royal Icing (see page 12)
4 finger biscuits
4 round yellow Liquorice All-sorts (for the hubcaps)
4 yellow crystallized jelly rings (for the wheel rims)

1. Make ladders using chocolate Matchmakers, trimmed and attached to each other with the melted chocolate.
2. Make two to three bells (see page 80) using caster sugar. When the bells are dry, paint them using the gold food colouring powder and non-toxic paint base.
3. Bake the loaf cake and when completely cool, place it on the thin board trimmed to fit the base of the cake.
4. Cut a 4 cm (1½ in) rectangular piece off the front of the cake and place it on top to form the cab of the fire engine (see illustration).

5. Brush the cake with the apricot glaze, using a pastry brush. Roll out the red fondant icing and completely cover the cake, gently rubbing down sections to achieve good adhesion and ensure a smooth surface. Remove the red window sections using a sharp knife and inlay the windows with rolled-out white fondant icing of the same thickness and size, using your fingers to smooth over the edges (see page 78).
6. Decorate the large cake board. Brush the intended roadway with egg white. Roll out the black fondant icing and place it on the prepared cake board.
7. Cut away excess black icing and edge the road with brown sugar (ground), green icing (grass) and the daisy bushes. Use the white cigarette sweets for dotted lines and pedestrian crossing.
8. Using melted chocolate, attach two pieces of flat liquorice to the fire engine for the front and back bumpers, and then place a small rectangle of white fondant icing, to represent the number plate. When the icing is dry, write your child's name and age on the number plate with a black food colouring pen.

9. Join 5 liquorice boot laces together with remaining melted chocolate to form the water hose and place on top of the engine, topped by a large ladder (see photograph). Attach the side ladders, the yellow Fruit Pastilles and the bell.
10. Draw in details such as the door outlines, handles, windscreen wipers and headlight surrounds, using a black food colouring pen or a piping bag fitted with a number 1 writing tube and filled with either black royal icing or melted chocolate.
11. Place the finger biscuits on the roadway in the axle positions and lower the fire engine (mounted on its small board) onto the larger cake board. Lastly, attach the round yellow Liquorice All-sorts (hubcaps) surrounded by crystallized jelly rings (rims) and an unwound liquorice boot lace to represent wheels.

Rugby Ball

EQUIPMENT

Oval rugby ball tin
Thin cake board cut to fit the base of the ball
Palette knife
Skewer
1 substitute piping bag (see page 75)
Number 2 writing tube
56 x 30 cm (22 x 12 in) rectangular cake board
2 piping bags
Sharp knife
Number 7 star tube

INGREDIENTS

¾ x Madeira or Oil Sponge Cake recipe, using 3 eggs (see page 6 or 7)
500 g (1 lb) Butter Icing (see page 12)
45 ml (3 tbsp) cocoa powder, sifted
Yellow food colouring
Liquorice strips cut into 3 cm (1¼ in) lengths (for laces)
125 g (4 oz) chocolate Butter Icing (see page 12)
1 kg (2 lb) white Fondant Icing (see page 11)
Green and black food colouring
Egg white
50 g (1¾ oz) white Royal Icing (see page 12)
4 large spiral rainbow candy sticks (for the goal posts)
2 rainbow candy bars (for the cross bars)
25 g (1 oz) white chocolate, melted
Ball candles

1. Make the Madeira or oil sponge cake and allow to cool completely.
2. Cut the thin cake board to fit the base of the cake. Place the rugby ball cake on this oval board.
3. Colour the butter icing with the sifted cocoa powder and a little yellow food colouring to achieve a caramel colour and then spread it over the ball.
4. Smooth the icing using a heated palette knife. Using a skewer, draw lines in the icing to resemble seams.
5. Place six liquorice laces across top of the ball. Pipe eyelets using the substitute piping bag, writing tube and a little of the chocolate butter icing.
6. Make holes in the rectangular cake board where the goal posts are to be positioned (see photograph).
7. Colour the white fondant icing with green and a touch of black food colouring (for the grass), and roll it out to a shape large enough to cover the cake board.
8. Brush the board with egg white then lift the green fondant icing onto the board, cutting away excess and smoothing the surface (see page 11). Prick the air bubbles with a pin and smooth away with your fingers. Locate the holes already made in the cake board for the goal posts and mark them, as well as the field lines, on the fondant icing, using pin marks.
9. Pipe white royal icing over the green fondant icing to indicate the lines on the rugby field, using a piping bag fitted with the writing tube (see page 77).
10. Insert the goal posts (candy sticks) through the holes in the cake board. Cut off excess under the board. Pipe around the base of each pole with royal icing.
11. Measure the distance between the goal posts and carefully adjust the length of the cross bars using a sharp knife. Join the cross bars to the posts, using melted white chocolate, which sets quickly.
12. Lift the ball onto the board and centre it on the field, being careful not to damage the white lines.
13. Using the remaining chocolate butter icing and the star tube, pipe stars (see page 76) around the base of the ball and secure the ball candles to the cake (rugby ball) and the board.

HAPPY
BIRTHDAY

Fishing in the Country

EQUIPMENT

2 piping bags
Number 5 star tube
23 cm (9 in) deep square tin
15 cm (6 in) deep small round tin
46 cm (18 in) square cake board
Plastic fish mould (optional)
Skewer
Fishing line
Palette knife
Grass or hair icing tube
Scissors
Plastic bushes and fencing
Plastic eagle and dairy cows

INGREDIENTS

50 g (1¾ oz) Fondant Icing (see page 11)
Food colouring of your choice
1.5 kg (3 lb) Butter Icing (see page 12)
2 ml (½ tsp) cocoa powder
1¼ x Oil Sponge Cake recipe, using 5 eggs (see page 7)
¾ x Oil Sponge Cake recipe, using 2–3 eggs (see page 7)
Jelly fish sweets or gums, or chocolate fish made with 50 g (2 oz) white chocolate
Turquoise food colouring powder
3 finger biscuits
25 g (⅞ oz) dark chocolate, melted
6 chocolate-coated finger biscuits
8 x 8 cm (3 x 3 in) rice paper (for the sail)
2 chocolate Matchmakers (for the mast and the fishing rod)
1 sour candy belt (for the flag)
Green food colouring
125 ml (½ cup) blue piping jelly (see page 78)
Green sour candy belt or angelica (for the reeds)
Rock candy (for the rocks)
Moulded yellow daisies (see page 79), optional

HANDY HINTS

1. Jelly fish are obtainable from sweet shops and daisy bunches from icing shops.
2. A plastic toy fisherman could be used to replace the edible fisherman.

1. Mould the sleeping fisherman in fondant icing (see page 80) and when dry, paint him using food colouring. Pipe his hat with the star tube and 25 ml (2 tbsp) of the butter icing coloured with the cocoa powder.
2. Make the large square and small round oil sponge cakes and when cool, position the larger cake to the rear of the cake board, leaving a 5 cm (2 in) edge. Cut the round cake in two sections and place one on either side of the square cake (see photograph).
3. If making your own fish, melt the white chocolate, tint it with turquoise food colouring powder and then pipe it into the plastic fish moulds to set (see page 81).
4. Make the raft by placing the three finger biscuits together, coating them in the melted dark chocolate and then covering them with the six chocolate-coated finger biscuits across their length. Pierce the rice paper sail with a sharp skewer and then thread the chocolate Matchmaker mast through the holes. Top the mast with a flag cut from a sour candy belt.
5. Using melted dark chocolate, attach mast securely to the raft, together with the sleeping fisherman and his Matchmaker fishing rod with its (inedible) fishing line.
6. Add green food colouring to remaining butter icing and spread half the icing over the cake and board.

7. Using a palette knife, spread the blue jelly diagonally across and down the front corner of the cake and onto the board to resemble a stream with a small waterfall (see photograph).
8. Fit the grass icing tube to the piping bag and fill it with the remaining green butter icing. Pipe the green icing to form grass on either side of the river banks.
9. Carefully position the raft complete with the sleeping fisherman on the blue jelly stream, surrounded by the jelly or chocolate fish. Insert the end of the fishing line into the stream. Slice the green sour candy belt or the angelica to make long, thin reeds, and then place these, together with the rock candy and the moulded daisies (if using), in position along the edge of the stream.
10. Finally, arrange all the plastic bushes and fences, the plastic eagle and the dairy cows around the cake and on the cake board to complete the fishing scene.

Fort

EQUIPMENT

28 x 10 x 11 cm (11 x 4 x 4½ in) loaf tin
23 cm (9 in) deep square cake tin
15 cm (6 in) deep square cake tin
46 cm (18 in) square cake board
Palette knife
Skewer
1 piping bag
5 mm (¼ in) large star tube
Sharp knife
Plastic soldiers and Red Indians
Flag

INGREDIENTS

3 x Oil Sponge Cake recipe, using 11 eggs (see page 7)
1½ kg (3 lb) Butter Icing (see page 12)
Black food colouring
Yellow sugar
White Liquorice All-sorts (for the barriers around the fort)
Brown wafer biscuits (for windows, door and drawbridge)
2 liquorice Liquoroos (for the cannons)
Liquorice All-sorts (for the cannons)
25 g (⅞ oz) dark chocolate, melted
Lifesaver sweets (for the wheels)
Blue piping jelly, for the moat (see page 78)
Egg white
Desiccated coconut
Green food colouring
Dark brown sugar (for the path)
Candles

1. Make one loaf and two square oil sponge cakes and leave them to cool completely before icing.
2. Position the larger square cake on the cake board. Divide the loaf cake into three and place one-third next to the medium-sized square cake on the second level, and the other third as the top level of the fort.
3. Colour the butter icing grey by mixing in black food colouring. Sandwich the levels of the fort together with grey butter icing.
4. Spread grey butter icing over the entire cake and smooth with a heated palette knife.
5. Using a skewer, draw lines on the fort walls to create the effect of large bricks.
6. Sprinkle the yellow sugar along the three flat levels of the fort. Using a star tube, pipe rosettes of grey butter icing around the base of the fort and on the edges of each level.
7. Cut the white Liquorice All-sorts in half and position upright around all the levels as a barrier.
8. Cut the wafer biscuits with a sharp knife and attach them to the fort walls to represent the windows, the front door and the drawbridge.
9. To make the cannons, cut the Liquoroos into three equal lengths and attach each to a large Liquorice All-sort, using melted chocolate. Attach the Lifesaver sweets to represent wheels (see photograph).
10. Colour the coconut with the green food colouring.
11. Spread the blue piping jelly carefully around the fort (for the moat), then brush the rest of the board with a little egg white and sprinkle with green coconut (the grass) followed by brown sugar (the pathway).
12. Complete the cake by positioning the plastic soldiers, the Red Indians, the flag and the candles.

HANDY HINT

Freeze the remaining one-third of the loaf cake or use it to make a trifle.

Red Indian Wigwam

EQUIPMENT

Dolly Varden (dome-shaped) tin
40 cm (16 in) oval cake board
Sharp knife
Palette knife
1 piping bag
Number 5 star tube
Tape measure
Plastic Red Indians, eagle and totem pole

INGREDIENTS

1 x Oil Sponge Cake recipe, using 4 eggs (see page 7)
2 wafer biscuits (for flap at entrance to wigwam)
600 g (1 lb 3½ oz) cream Butter Icing (see page 12)
20 ml (4 tsp) cocoa powder
1 finger biscuit (for the canoe)
Green candy straws
Mini Liquorice All-sorts
Orange jellybeans
Liquorice comforts
3 chocolate Matchmakers
Egg white
Yellow sugar (for the sand)
Clear piping jelly (see page 78)
Blue and green food colouring
Rock candy (for the rocks)
3 Flake chocolate bars (for the logs)
Candyfloss (optional)

1. Make the oil sponge cake in the Dolly Varden dome-shaped tin and allow to cool completely.
2. Position the cake a little to one side on the cake board and, using a sharp knife, remove a small slice from the cake to represent the wigwam's entrance.
3. Position the tapered wafer biscuits (representing the flap to the entrance of the wigwam) on one side, using a little butter icing.
4. Colour 500 g (1 lb) of the icing with 15 ml (1 tbsp) of the cocoa powder, and 50 g (1¾ oz) of the icing with the remaining 5 ml (1 tsp) cocoa powder. Spread the lighter chocolate icing over the wigwam cake and smooth it using a heated palette knife.
5. Pipe the darker chocolate butter icing around the finger biscuit to form a canoe, using the star tube.
6. Spread the remainder of the darker chocolate butter icing over the entrance to the wigwam (the part where the small slice was removed).
7. Using the tape measure, divide the wigwam into six equal sections. Place candy straws extending from the top ring down to the base of the cake (see photograph). Decorate the sides with the Liquorice All-sorts and jellybeans, and the top with the liquorice comforts and chocolate Matchmakers.
8. To decorate the area around the wigwam, spread a little egg white over the cake board and sprinkle it with yellow sugar to represent sand.
9. Colour the piping jelly with the blue colouring and the remaining butter icing with the green colouring. Use a palette knife to apply the blue piping jelly (the river) and green butter icing (the grass).
10. Place the rock candy, the Flake chocolate bars, the canoe and the plastic decorations on the board. Just before serving, remove the candyfloss from its bag and position it on top of the wigwam so that it looks as if there is smoke coming from within the tent.

Army Tank

EQUIPMENT

28 x 10 x 11 cm (11 x 4 x 4½ in) loaf tin
Sharp knife
40 cm (16 in) oval cake board
Palette knife
1 piping bag
Number 3 writing tube
Plastic soldiers

INGREDIENTS

1 x Oil Sponge Cake recipe, using 4 eggs (see page 7)
500 g (1 lb) Butter Icing (see page 12)
Green, yellow and black food colouring
8 strands flat liquorice
12 liquorice catherine wheels
1 liquorice boot lace (for the flap guarding the entrance to the turret)
1 rainbow candy stick (for the barrel)
100 g (3½ oz) Butter Icing (see page 12)
Green and black food colouring
Egg white
Yellow sugar (for desert sand)

1. Make the loaf-shaped oil sponge cake and leave to cool completely before cutting.
2. Colour the 500 g (1 lb) butter icing with the green, yellow and black colouring to make it army green.
3. Cut the cake in half vertically, but only to half the depth, then cut away to the front. Cut this section into four lengths and place along each side of the cake, using butter icing to secure the lengths into position (see illustration).
4. Gently shave the sides of the top cake (the turret) so that it tapers to meet the front and side sections.

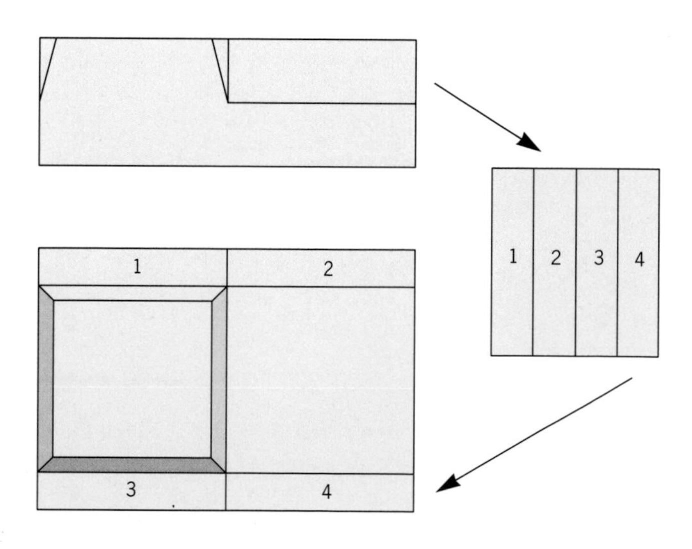

5. Place the cake on the cake board and then cover it completely in army green butter icing. Smooth the icing using a heated palette knife.
6. Place the flat liquorice strands in position over the sides of the iced cake. Place liquorice catherine wheels on the sides of the cake, and then the liquorice boot lace on the top of the cake (turret).
7. Insert the rainbow candy stick (barrel) into the cake.
8. Colour the 100 g (3½ oz) butter icing dark green with the green and black food colouring.
9. Pipe the dots (see page 77) in dark green to outline the shape of the tank (see photograph).
10. Brush the cake board with egg white and sprinkle yellow sugar (the sand) around the base of the tank.
11. Decorate the cake board and the tank with the plastic soldiers.

HANDY HINT

Ensure that the candy stick (barrel) is inserted deeply into the cake (tank) to make sure that it holds its angle without flopping down onto the cake.

Basket Weave Hat

EQUIPMENT
15 cm (6 in) round domed cake tin
36 cm (14 in) round cake board
2 piping bags
Number 3 writing tube
Basket weave icing tube
Scissors
1.2 m (50 in) white satin ribbon

INGREDIENTS
½ x Oil Sponge Cake recipe, using 2 eggs (see page 7)
1.5 kg (3 lb) Butter Icing (see page 12)
Yellow food colouring
16 white marshmallows
16 yellow Jelly Tots

1. Make the round domed oil sponge cake and allow it to cool completely.
2. Centre the cake on the cake board.
3. Colour the butter icing with the yellow food colouring.
4. Spread yellow butter icing smoothly and thinly over the cake (hat's crown) and the cake board (hat's brim).
5. Fit the two piping bags with the writing tube and the basket weave icing tube and fill with yellow butter icing. Commence the basket weave (see page 77), starting from the central base of the crown and then working towards each side.
6. When you have finished the crown, refill the piping bags with yellow butter icing and continue the basket weave, spiralling out from the crown to the edge of the brim, so that the brim is completely covered.
7. Using the number 3 writing tube, pipe a row of dots (see page 77) around the brim to neaten the edge.
8. Using the scissors, make marshmallow flowers (see page 82) and attach a yellow Jelly Tot to the centre of each flower.
9. Attach the flowers to the brim of the hat by first placing one flower each at the 12, 6, 9 and 3 o'clock positions. Now fill in the remaining flowers, using two flowers for each quarter of the cake.
10. The next day, when the icing has hardened, tie the ribbon around the base of the crown, forming a bow.

HANDY HINTS

1. Marshmallow flower petals can be coloured by dipping the sticky cut edge into coloured hundreds and thousands or jelly powder.
2. A round metal pudding bowl can be used as the cake tin for the crown of the hat.

Princess Peach

EQUIPMENT

Dolly Varden (dome-shaped) tin
36 cm (14 in) round cake board
Palette knife
2 straight petal icing tubes
3 piping bags
Number 2 writing tube
Doll with a skewer base (sometimes provided with the Dolly Varden tin), or use a Barbie-like doll
Plastic-and-lace umbrella and fan (optional)

INGREDIENTS

1 x Oil Sponge Cake recipe, using 4 eggs (see page 7)
1 kg (2 lb) vanilla Butter Icing (see page 12)
Yellow and red food colouring
Gold balls (for the princess's necklace)
6 peach lollipops (for posts around the cake board)
18 tangerine Fizz bars (for balustrading around the cake board)
Champagne candles

1. Make the oil sponge cake mixture and bake it in the Dolly Varden tin.
2. When completely cool, centre the cake (which forms the skirt of the doll) on the cake board.
3. Colour half the vanilla butter icing peach, using yellow and red food colouring.
4. Cover the cake with white icing, smoothing the surface with a palette knife.
5. Insert the petal icing tubes into two of the piping bags and fill one bag with white and one with peach icing.
6. Starting at the base of the cake, pipe a row of peach petals. Curl the tube round so that you make half-circle petal shapes.
7. Follow the peach row with a row of white petals, and continue until you reach the waist.
8. Insert the skewer of the doll inside the cake (so that only her top half shows above the cake) and then wedge the umbrella and fan (if used) into the fingers of the doll.
9. Pipe the bodice with alternating rows of small frills using the same tubes, or with dots (see page 77) using the writing tube and the third piping bag filled with peach butter icing.
10. Complete the bodice straps with the same peach dots. Pipe dots around the neck. Attach the gold balls to the dots to make the princess's necklace.
11. Cover the cake board with the remaining peach butter icing, and smooth it using a palette knife dipped in boiling water.
12. Decorate the edge of the cake board with inverted peach lollipops to represent the posts of a platform – one for each year of the child's age.
13. Just before serving the cake, curl the Fizz bars (see page 82) and place them between the peach lollipops to represent balustrading and to act as a support for the candles (use butter icing to attach the candles to the Fizz bars).

HANDY HINT

Position the arms of the doll before the bodice is iced. This prevents the icing from breaking off when dry, due to unnecessary movement.

Sunflower

EQUIPMENT

23 cm (9 in) round cake tin
40 cm (16 in) round cake board
Sunflower template (see page 86)
Sharp knife
Palette knife
5 mm (¼ in) large star tube
1 piping bag
1 substitute piping bag (see page 75)

INGREDIENTS

½ x Oil Sponge or Madeira Cake recipe, using 2 eggs (see page 6 or 7)
1 kg (2 lb) Butter Icing (see page 12)
Yellow food colouring
Edible orange glitter
Black seeded sweets (for sunflower seeds)
Green candy straws (for stem and leaves of flower)
Green piping jelly, for the leaves (see page 78)
Chocolate bees (see page 14) or fondant butterflies

1. Make a round oil sponge or Madeira cake and allow it to cool completely before cutting it. Place the cake on the cake board.
2. Using the template and a sharp knife, cut the petalled edge around the sunflower cake.
3. Colour the butter icing with the yellow food colouring.
4. Spread yellow butter icing over the entire cake, using the palette knife.
5. Fit the star tube into the piping bag and then fill it with the remaining yellow butter icing. Pipe individual petals, working from the outside towards the inside, ending in the centre.
6. Pipe straight lines (using the same piping bag and star tube) from the top of the petals to the board.
7. Neaten the bottom of the cake with a row of stars (see page 76), using the same piping bag.
8. Dust the inside edge of the sunflower petals with the edible orange glitter.
9. Fill in the centre of the cake with the black seeded sweets to represent sunflower seeds.
10. Arrange the green candy straws on the cake board, using one for the stem and the other three shaped to form leaves. The tips of the candy straws will usually keep together if firmly pressed.
11. Fill in the surface of the leaves with the green piping jelly, using the substitute piping bag. Finally, complete the cake by placing the chocolate bees, the fondant butterflies or the ladybirds (see page 65) on the cake board around the sunflower.

HANDY HINT

If you are unable to find edible glitter at a cake icing shop, you can make your own by combining 45 ml (3½ tbsp) hot water (colour the water if desired) with 20 g (40 ml, ¾ oz, 3 tbsp) gum arabic and stirring this over hot water until dissolved. Brush the mixture onto a clean baking tray and place in a warm oven at 120 °C (250 °F) until dry. Scrape the dry glitter off the baking tray and crush into fine flakes with a rolling pin. Store the glitter in an airtight container.

Happy Birthday

Enchanted Tree House

EQUIPMENT

18 cm (7 in) deep round cake tin
14 cm (5½ in) deep round cake tin or 13 cm (5 in) ice-cream bombe tin (an upright tin with tapered sides)
40 cm (16 in) round cake board
Sharp knife
1 piping bag
Number 2 writing tube
2 substitute piping bags (see page 75)
Number 5 star tube
Black food colouring pen

INGREDIENTS

1½ x Madeira Cake recipe, using 5 eggs (see page 8)
750 g (1½ lb) chocolate Butter Icing (see page 12)
50 g (1¾ oz) Butter Icing (see page 12)
Yellow food colouring
Strawberry sour candy straws (for the front door)
Wafer biscuits, cream and chocolate
12 large Flake chocolate bars
125 g (4 oz) white chocolate, melted
Red food colouring powder
7 Sweetie Pies
7 white marshmallows
Liquorice All-sorts
Black gums
Dark chocolate, melted
Pink Jelly Tots
Egg white
Green coconut (for the grass)
Brown sugar (for the path)
Store-bought coconut mushroom sweets and lollipops
Miniature daisy bunches (see page 79)
Store-bought fondant butterflies and jelly worms

1. Make the two round cakes and when completely cool place the smaller cake on top of the larger one. Place the cakes on the board. Using a sharp knife, shave the edges of the cake to create an even-sloped tree.
2. Place the wedges on top of the tree, to support the wafer roof of the tree house, or use two Sweetie Pies.
3. Sandwich the two cakes together and cover them in chocolate butter icing, leaving spaces for the yellow windows. Colour the 50 g (1¾ oz) butter icing with the yellow food colouring and use this to fill the window areas. Pipe the window panes using a little of the chocolate icing and the writing tube. Make the door using candy straws, and wedge a chocolate wafer biscuit (awning) into the cake above the door.
4. Place the Flake chocolate bars at the top of the tree (branches) and at the base (roots).
5. Break up remaining Flake chocolate bars and attach pieces to the chocolate butter icing (for bark effect).
6. Taper the cream wafers over the front (attic area) and cover the roof using chocolate wafers.
7. Colour 100 g (3½ oz) of the melted white chocolate with the red food colouring powder. Make the toadstools by coating the Sweetie Pies with melted red chocolate. Using melted white chocolate, attach the Sweetie Pies to the white marshmallows (bases of the toadstools). Decorate the tops of the toadstools with melted white chocolate dots and little windows (cut from the yellow fondant of Liquorice All-sorts). Use a

black food colouring pen to draw in the little window panes on the toadstools.

8. Make the strawberry liquorice ladybirds by attaching the black gums to the strawberry liquorice tubes and then piping them with the melted dark chocolate, using a substitute piping bag.
9. Finish off the roof and the attic area of the enchanted tree house with the pink Jelly Tots, a round strawberry Liquorice All-sort and finally the piped yellow icing, using the star tube (see photograph).
10. Brush the cake board around the base of the tree with egg white, then sprinkle with green coconut (for the grass) and brown sugar (for the path) and use some of the following sweets: mushroom lollipops, coconut mushrooms, daisy bunches, fondant butterflies, jelly worms, ladybirds and toadstools.

Present Cake

EQUIPMENT

20 cm (8 in) deep square cake tin
30 cm (12 in) square cake board
Non-stick baking paper
'Happy Birthday' sign or food colouring pen
Star cutter
Pastry brush
Sharp scissors

INGREDIENTS

1 x Oil Sponge or Madeira Cake recipe, using 4 eggs (see page 6 or 7)
500 g (1 lb) vanilla Butter Icing (see page 12) or 125 ml (4 fl oz, ½ cup) Apricot Glaze (see page 13)
1½ kg (3 lb) Fondant Icing (see page 11)
Yellow and blue food colouring
White vegetable fat
Egg white
Edible orange glitter (see page 62)
Icing sugar

1. Make a square oil sponge or Madeira cake and allow it to cool completely.
2. Centre the cake on the cake board and spread the butter icing smoothly over the cake, or brush the cake with the apricot glaze.
3. Make a card for the present using a little fondant icing. Roll out the fondant icing, then cut it into a rectangle and dry it flat on non-stick baking paper. When the card is completely dry, attach a 'Happy Birthday' sign to it, or write your own message on it using a food colouring pen.
4. Colour one-third of the fondant icing with yellow food colouring. Roll it out thinly on a smooth surface greased with white vegetable fat and cut out the ribbons 2.5 cm (1 in) wide. Set aside the ribbons, re-roll the remainder of the yellow fondant and cut out the stars, using the star cutter. Brush the stars with egg white, sprinkle with orange glitter and set aside until they are completely dry.
5. Colour the remaining two-thirds of the fondant icing with blue colouring. Knead the fondant icing well and then roll it out on the surface (which has been dusted with icing sugar) to a square shape that will fit over the cake and the sides.
6. Lift the fondant icing over the cake and smooth it down. Form folds on the two sides (as would be the case with a wrapped gift).
7. Using a pastry brush, brush a little egg white across the cake in the position where the ribbon is going to lie. Carefully place the ribbon over the band of egg white, tucking the ends under the fondant (wrapping paper) on each side.
8. Brush the back of the stars with egg white and place them evenly over the cake.
9. Make the bow with the excess yellow fondant ribbon. Use a pair of scissors to make the fish tail ends to the ribbons, then place them together with the inscribed card on the present.

HANDY HINT

Alternatively you could make a card with rice paper and write a message on it with food colouring pens.

Happy Birthday

Mermaid

EQUIPMENT

Mermaid doll (if not decorating your own doll) or use a Barbie-like doll
Plastic mould for sea horses (optional)
36 cm (14 in) round cake tin
46 cm (18 in) round cake board
2 piping bags
Number 3 writing tube
Star tube or shell tube
Plastic fish candle holders

INGREDIENTS

125 g (4 oz) white Fondant Icing (see page 11)
Pink and blue food colouring
Silver balls (edible)
Egg white
Edible white glitter (see page 62)
100 g (3½ oz) white chocolate, melted
Turquoise food colouring
1½ x Oil Sponge Cake recipe, using 6 eggs (see page 7)
500 g (1 lb) vanilla Butter Icing (see page 12)
1 kg (2 lb) Fondant Icing (see page 11)
200 g (7 oz) white Royal Icing (see page 12)
Blue piping jelly (for the sea)
Blue rock candy (for the rocks)
Jelly fish or gums
Brown sugar (for the beach)

1. If making your own mermaid, dress the doll using white fondant icing mixed with pink and blue food colouring (to produce a lilac colour).
2. Mould the tail. Thin out the icing once you reach the doll's feet so that you can make the tail fin (it should taper towards the end). Make the fish scales using the tip of a teaspoon. Use scraps of lilac fondant icing to make the mermaid's top. Decorate her waist with silver balls gently embedded in the fondant.
3. Brush the mermaid's scales with egg white and sprinkle with edible white glitter.
4. Make sea horses using the melted white chocolate tinted with turquoise food colouring and piping it into a plastic mould (see page 81).
5. Make the cake and, when completely cool, centre it on the cake board and spread vanilla butter icing over it.
6. Roll out the fondant icing so that it is large enough to cover the entire cake. Gently lift the fondant icing and place it over the cake, easing away fullness around the edges. Smooth the fondant icing by gently rubbing it to the surface of the cake (see page 11).
7. Fit the piping bags with a shell and writing tube respectively, and fill with prepared white royal icing.
8. Using the shell tube, pipe shellwork (see page 77) around the base of the cake and, using the writing tube, pipe seaweed shapes at regular intervals around the side. Leave to dry before continuing.
9. Attach sea horses or jelly fish to the sides of the cake with royal icing. Spread half the top with blue piping jelly dotted with rock candy and jelly fish.
10. Sprinkle brown sugar over the rest of the cake and the board. Place mermaid on a piece of rock candy.

HANDY HINT

The mermaid's tail must be moulded and left to dry in a sitting position. Seat the mermaid on a container, similar in height to the rock candy, to allow her tail to dry.

Happy
Birthday

Queen of Hearts

EQUIPMENT

Heart, club, diamond and spade cutters
Non-stick baking paper, pencil and pins
33 x 23 x 5 cm (13 x 9 x 2 in) rectangular cake tin
46 cm (18 in) square cake board
Queen of Hearts template (see page 87)
Blue food colouring pen
Food colouring paste (red, yellow, blue)
Paintbrushes (fine and medium)
2 piping bags
Number 7 star tube
Number 2 writing tube

INGREDIENTS

1½ kg (3 lb) white Fondant Icing (see page 11)
Red and black food colouring, or ready-made
25 g (1 oz) red fondant icing (hearts, diamonds) and
25 g (1 oz) black fondant icing (spades, clubs)
1¼ x Madeira Cake recipe, using 5 eggs (see page 6)
125 ml (4 fl oz, ½ cup) Apricot Glaze (see page 13)
1 kg (2 lb) marzipan
Egg white
Royal Icing, using 2 egg whites (see page 12)
Gold food colouring powder and non-toxic paint base
Heart candles

1. Remove about 50 g (2 oz) of the fondant icing and colour one half of this amount red and the other half black using food colouring (or use ready-made red and black fondant icing). Roll out the coloured fondant icing and, using cutters, cut out nine hearts and nine diamonds in red and nine clubs and nine spades in black. Allow these shapes to dry flat on the non-stick baking paper. Keep the remaining fondant icing in an airtight plastic bag.
2. Make the rectangular Madeira cake and allow it to cool completely.
3. Brush cake with apricot glaze and cover with marzipan. Brush marzipan with egg white and cover with three-quarters of the white fondant icing, smoothing the surface and cutting off the excess (see page 11).
4. The following day, when the icing has set slightly, transfer the details of the Queen of Hearts template to the surface of the icing.
5. Centre the template on the cake and secure the four corners using pins. Gently prick out the design. Remove the template and join the pin pricks with the tip of a pin or lightly with a food colouring pen.
6. Paint the Queen of Hearts directly onto the icing, starting from one end and working down. When dry, outline the fine areas using a blue food colouring pen.
7. Roll out the remaining white fondant icing and cut the frame to fit around the top edge of the card.
8. Use royal icing to attach the frame with mitred corners to the top edges of the cake. Form lines over the surface of the frame using the back of a knife.
9. Pipe stars (see page 76) around the base of the cake and around the edge of the frame, using white royal icing and the star tube. Using the writing tube and royal icing, pipe 'Happy Birthday' on the frame.
10. When writing is dry, brush the frame with gold food colouring powder dipped in the non-toxic paint base.
11. Attach the heart, diamond, club and spade cut-outs around the sides of the cake using royal icing.

HANDY HINT

To avoid smudging, make sure the painting of the Queen of Hearts is completely dry before completing the icing on the cake.

HAPPY
BIRTHDAY

Christmas Tree

EQUIPMENT

1 nylon piping bag
17 mm (¾ in) large plain tube
Non-stick baking paper
Baking sheet
Holly cutter
Brown food colouring pen
1 substitute piping bag (see page 75)
33 x 23 x 5 cm (13 x 9 x 2 in) rectangular cake tin
Christmas tree template (see page 86)
46 cm (18 in) square or oval cake board
Palette knife or fork
Holly and berries

INGREDIENTS

2 egg whites (produces 8–10 meringue snowmen)
Pinch of salt
125 ml (100 g, 3½ oz, ½ cup) caster sugar
50 g (1¾ oz) Fondant Icing (see page 11)
Green and red food colouring powder
White vegetable fat
Green fondant or candy belts (for the scarves)
Red Jelly Tots (for the gloves)
50 g (1¾ oz) chocolate, melted
Snowman's top hat candles
1 x Oil Sponge Cake recipe, using 4 eggs (see page 7)
750 g (1½ lb) green Butter Icing (see page 12)
Sweets and edible balls (for tree lights and decorations)
2 Flake chocolate bars (for the tree trunk)
Chocolate Sweetie Pie (for the inside of the barrel)
11 chocolate-coated finger biscuits (for the covering of the barrel)
White Royal Icing, using 2 egg whites (see page 12)

1. To make the meringue snowmen, first set the oven temperature to 110 °C (225 °C).
2. Whisk the egg whites with a pinch of salt until foamy, but not dry. Gradually add the caster sugar, beating the mixture until it is stiff and shiny.
3. Fit the nylon piping bag with the large plain tube and fill it with the meringue mixture. Pipe the snowmen (first the base, then the head and the arms) onto the non-stick baking paper on a baking sheet. Bake on the middle shelf of the preheated oven for 2½ hours and leave to cool in the oven.
4. Colour three-quarters of the fondant icing with the green food colouring powder and roll out thinly on a smooth surface greased with white vegetable fat. Cut out the snowmen's scarves and the holly leaves (using a holly cutter). Colour the remaining fondant icing red and roll this into berries. Leave to dry.
5. Decorate the snowmen (when they are completely cold) with green fondant or candy belt scarves, Jelly Tot gloves, facial features (either piped in melted chocolate or drawn using the brown food colouring pen) and top hat candles. Use melted chocolate to attach these decorations to the snowmen. Store the meringue snowmen in an airtight container.
6. Make a rectangular oil sponge cake and allow to cool completely before cutting the tree shape using the template provided.
7. Place the Christmas tree cake on the cake board and spread the entire surface with green butter icing.
8. Roughen the icing, using a fork or palette knife, to give the effect of a fir tree.
9. Decorate the cake with a selection of sweets and edible balls to resemble Christmas decorations and Christmas tree lights.

10. Cut the Flake chocolate bars and place them at the base of the tree (for the tree trunk).
11. Invert the Sweetie Pie and place it on its side. Using the melted chocolate, attach the chocolate-coated finger biscuits around the sides and the base of the Sweetie Pie (to create the effect of a barrel).
12. Spread the board with white royal icing (for the snow) and pipe small amounts over the tree, the holly and the snowmen's hats using a substitute piping bag.
13. Remove the snowmen from the airtight container and position them, together with the holly and berries, around the tree just before serving.

Decorating Equipment

With a few simple tools you can create stunning effects when decorating cakes. As your skills develop, more specialized pieces of equipment may be bought at cake icing shops. Some basic icing tools that make decorating cakes much easier and more pleasurable are listed below.

THE ICING TURNTABLE

Here the cake revolves on a turntable, making piping and decorating easier, especially on the sides of a round cake. It is ideal for heavy cakes as it allows easy access to all sides of the cake.

THE SMALL ROLLING PIN

This is useful when you need to roll out small amounts of fondant icing.

CAKE BOARDS

Always use a cake board as a base for your cake. It makes decorating much easier if you have a stable board on which to work. Cake boards are available in two thicknesses and in a variety of shapes.

ICING TUBES OR NOZZLES

There are many shapes and sizes from which to choose. With children's cakes, though, you will use mainly writing and star tubes, either large (measured in millimetres or inches) or small (identified by a number).

DISPOSABLE PLASTIC ICING BAGS

These bags are essential for piped work. They can be used with their plastic tip removed or with a large or small icing tube inserted.

PAINTBRUSHES

Use good quality brushes of varying sizes. These are obtainable at cake icing shops and art supply stores.

CRIMPING TOOLS

These come in different shapes that produce different patterns when crimping or pinching the fondant icing.

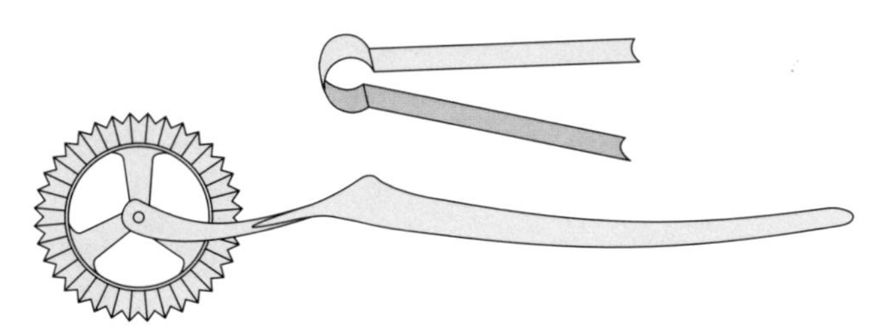

STAMENS, FLORIST'S TAPE AND WIRE

This equipment is essential for making bunches of daisies and can be bought from cake icing shops, together with the ready-made bunches of daisies.

NON-STICK BAKING PAPER

This is used to transfer templates onto cakes and it also acts as a base for floodwork and some piped work. It is ideal for lining cake tins prior to baking.

METAL OR PLASTIC CUTTERS AND PLUNGERS

These are used to make regular floral and other shapes.

PALETTE KNIFE

This is an essential tool for spreading icing over a cake.

FOOD COLOURING PENS

These provide an edible outline for painted work on a cake covered with fondant icing. They are also useful for drawing in fine features, for example faces, and writing messages on a cake, for example 'Happy Birthday'.

MODELLING TOOLS

They are very useful when modelling shapes and small areas in fondant icing or ice-cream.

FOOD COLOURING

Liquid, paste and powders can be used in all the icings and for paintwork. However, to avoid curdling when working with chocolate, only food powder can be used in conjunction with non-toxic paint bases that are obtainable from most cake icing shops. The amount of colouring used depends on the strength of colour required.

ICING COMBS

Plain and serrated combs create decorative effects on the sides of cakes where soft icings such as butter icing and royal icing have been used. A smooth, flat finish is achieved on the sides of cakes when using a plain comb, whereas all kinds of 'combed' pattern designs occur when using a serrated comb.

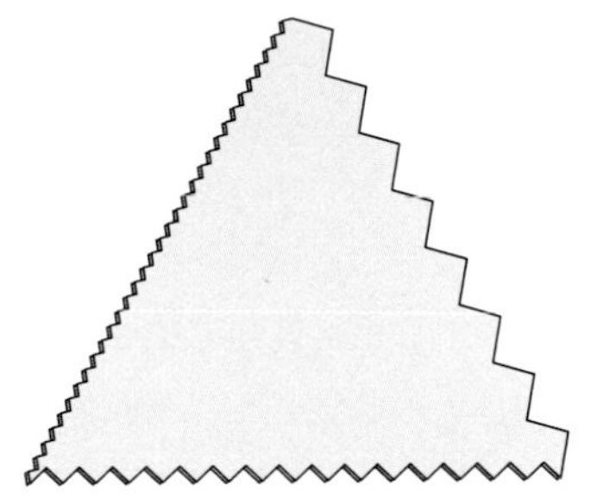

CANDLES

All of the candles used in this book were bought at kitchenware shops and departments, cake icing shops, stationers, toy shops and supermarkets.

Piping Bags

PLASTIC DISPOSABLE PIPING BAGS

These are now available in cake icing and kitchenware shops. These piping bags save time and are much stronger than the traditional greaseproof piping bags. There are usually two parts to a piping bag: the piping tube and the piping bag itself. If the piping tube is carefully removed after icing is completed and the plastic bag is washed in warm soapy water and then dried, you will find that you will be able to use the bags frequently, which makes them very economical indeed.

When working with chocolate, fill the disposable bag with melted chocolate, remembering to remove the tip of the bag only just before you begin piping. Should the chocolate begin to show signs of setting while you are working, place the plastic disposable bag in the microwave and heat on a low setting for a few seconds. This will melt the chocolate in the bag, and in so doing will enable you to continue using the same piping bag.

NYLON PIPING BAGS

These are ideal when you are using large tubes or piping large quantities of cream or meringue. Nylon piping bags can also be used for piping butter icing, but do not overfill as the heat of your hands causes the butter in the icing to melt slightly and the icing to break up. If you are going to use this type of piping bag for butter icing, rather refill the piping bag at regular intervals with smaller amounts of the icing mixture.

SUBSTITUTE PIPING BAGS

When only a minimal amount of piping is to be done on a cake, a substitute bag in the form of a strong plastic bag can be used. Ensure that the mixture to be piped is of a relatively soft consistency, for example whipped cream, butter icing, royal icing or melted chocolate.

When working with melted chocolate, pour the chocolate towards one of the bottom corners of the bag. Fold over the sides then the top corners of the bag. Snip the chocolate corner and pipe directly before the chocolate begins to harden.

When using a piping tube in the substitute bag, snip off one of the plastic bag's bottom corners and drop in the piping tube. Secure the bag to the piping tube using a few pieces of masking tape in the area of the tube. Fill the plastic bag and then close by folding over the sides and the top edge. When the piped work has been completed, remove the tube for washing before discarding the substitute piping bag.

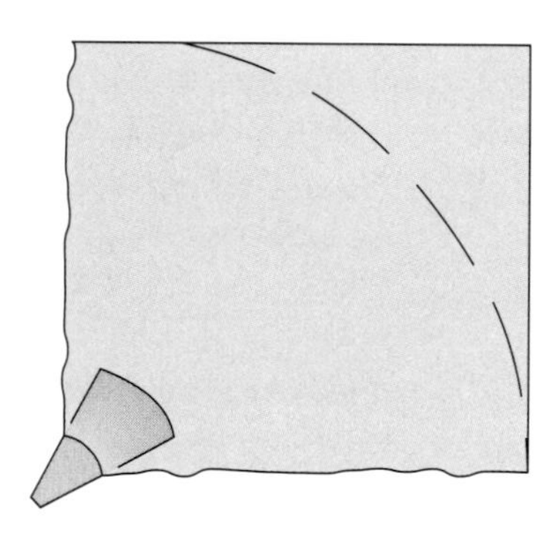

FILLING A PIPING BAG

1. Plastic disposable bags should have their tips removed to accommodate the piping tube. Only a quarter of the piping tube should be exposed when the icing is in position in the bag.
2. When you have placed the piping tube in the bag, roll down the sides (to the outside), supporting the piping tube section with your left hand.
3. Using a palette knife, fill the bag and direct the icing towards the icing tube.
4. Do not overfill the bags as this makes it difficult to control the piping bag when piping.
5. Unfold the sides of the piping bag to its full size and press the top edges of the bag together, then fold the corners in and roll the top down to rest against the contained icing. This prevents icing from oozing out of the top of the piping bag during the piping process.

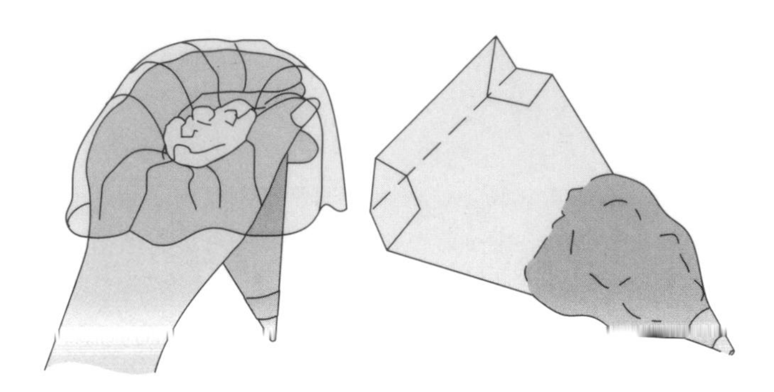

HOLDING A PIPING BAG

1. Ensure that your hands are clean and dry to prevent them slipping on the piping bag, thereby reducing your control over the piping bag.
2. Place the bag across your fingers in the palm of your right hand. Apply pressure with the thumb against the fingers to release the icing.
3. While cushioning the bag in your right hand, press mainly with the thumb on the top of the bag for the icing to flow, and lift the thumb to stop the flow.

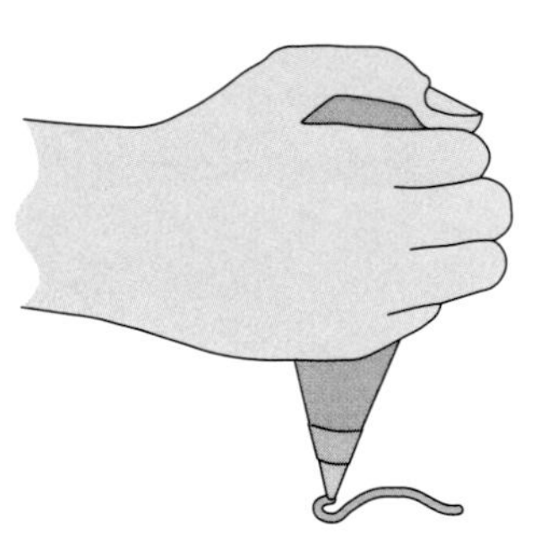

DIFFERENT TYPES OF PIPING

First organize your working area so that everything you require is close at hand. The angle at which you are working must feel comfortable, or the results will not be rewarding. The bag can be held straight or at an angle, depending on the shape you are piping.

PIPING A STAR

Choose a star tube to suit the size of the design. Hold the piping bag upright over the area to be iced and gently squeeze the bag to release the icing and form a star. The size of the star is governed by the size of the tube and the amount of icing squeezed out. Pull the tube off quickly, keeping the bag upright to give a neat point to the star. Maintain the same pressure to ensure uniformity in stars.

PIPING DOTS

Using any writing tube of your choice (either number 1, 2, 3 or 4), hold the piping bag directly over the area to be piped, gently applying a little pressure to the bag to form the dot. Release the pressure on the bag and move the end of the tube away towards the side of the dot so as not to form a sharp point, unless this effect is desired.

PIPING SHELLS

Use a shell tube or a star tube for this type of piping. Holding the piping bag at a 45° angle, place the tip of the tube against the surface to be worked on (the cake or the cake board). Gently squeeze out the icing while you lift the tube up slightly and then down again onto the cake or cake board, pulling off to release the icing. Repeat this procedure at the beginning where the last shell ended, ensuring that the untidy start of the shell does not show. Continue in this way.

PIPING LINES

Writing tubes of varying widths are available – the smaller the number, the finer the line will be.

For straight lines, start piping by gently resting the tip of the tube against the cake. Holding the bag at an angle, apply pressure to the bag and lift it slightly as you work. Continue to pipe, allowing the thread of piping to fall in a straight line. Do not pull, as this will cause the thread to break off. When the line is complete, allow the tube to rest on the surface of the cake and gently pull away, which will break the thread of icing.

For curved lines or for writing, it is a very good idea to practise first, before applying the piping directly to the finished cake. If printing, pipe the middle letters first and then work towards the sides to ensure that the writing is centred on the cake.

To make sharp points, stop and start at the end of a point, unlike you would for curved lines.

Basket Weave

This technique requires you to keep a constant pressure on the icing bag so that you do not get sudden splurges or widened lines.

INSTRUCTIONS

Prepare two piping bags:

1. One bag with a plain writing tube (number 2, 3 or 4).
2. One bag with a fitted basket-weave tube (the size of the tubes depends upon the size of the object to be covered with basket weave).

METHOD

1. Using the writing tube, pipe a straight line directly onto the iced cake.
2. Pipe short basket-weave lines at right angles to the straight line (consult the illustration to guide you), leaving a space the width of the tip of the basket-weave tube between each line.
3. Using the bag fitted with the plain tube, pipe a second straight line at right angles to the basket weave.
4. Using the bag fitted with the basket-weave tube, pipe a second set of short lines in the spaces between the first set. Continue until the required area is filled.

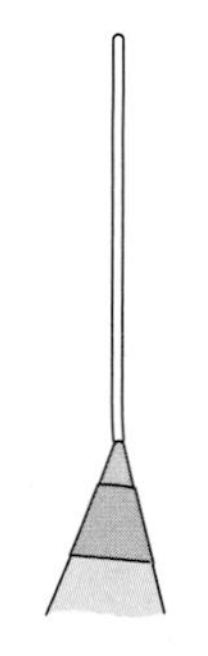

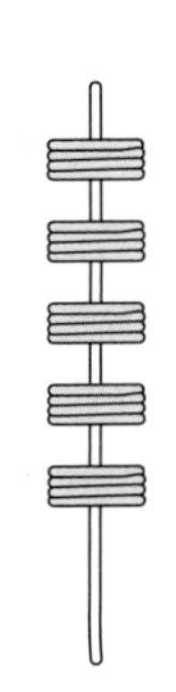

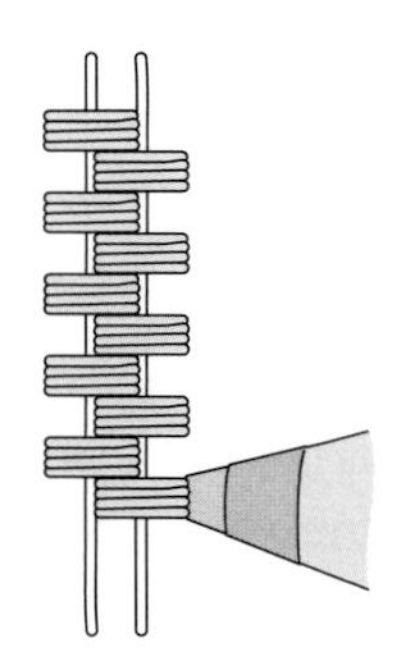

Piping Jelly

This type of jelly provides an easy and colourful method of decorating ice-cream as well as royal, fondant and butter icings. Piping jelly is available in colours such as red, green, yellow and clear, but these colours can be changed by using food colouring (e.g. blue liquid food colouring mixed with clear jelly produces the effect of water on a cake).

METHOD

1. Transfer the pattern to the surface of the cake that you are going to pipe, or pipe a freehand pattern, depending on the degree of difficulty of the chosen pattern and its size.
2. Pipe the outlines – use melted chocolate outlines on ice-cream, and royal or butter icing outlines on cakes. However, it is not essential to have an outline on these cakes as the jelly does not run unless it is piped onto a sloping surface.
3. Fill piping bag with jelly, remove the tip of the piping bag and pipe jelly onto the design shape. Alternatively, spread jelly over the design by using a palette knife.
4. Use a new piping bag for each colour jelly you use.
5. Piping jelly works very well for writing (e.g. 'Happy Birthday') because it has just the right consistency.

NOTE

Piping jelly does not harden, and children enjoy the taste as well as the vibrancy of the colours.

Inlaid Icing

Use this icing technique to make the windows of the fire engine cake (see page 46).

METHOD

1. Inlaid icing must be cut soon after the fondant icing has been put over the cake, before it dries.
2. Place the template design on non-stick baking paper over the fondant icing on the cake and prick out the template shape using a pin.
3. Use a sharp knife to cut out and remove the fondant icing shape from the cake.
4. Roll out a piece of fondant icing in a contrasting colour to the same thickness on a smooth surface greased with white vegetable fat, and use the template again to prick out the same shape that has been removed from the main cake.
5. Carefully cut out the new fondant icing shape and then inlay it back on the cake, making sure that it fits exactly into the shape on the cake. Using your finger, smooth over the join between the two pieces of fondant icing until the two edges meet exactly and the small dents disappear.

NOTE

When inlaying other small and simple shapes, you can use a biscuit cutter to cut out the sections from the fondant icing covering the cake and then use the same biscuit cutter again to cut the replacement shapes from the contrasting fondant icing.

Edible Paintwork

Food colouring is available in liquid, paste or powder form and can be used in the same way as you would use water colours (i.e. mix your paint by adding water to the food colouring paste or powder). Similarly, food colouring pens can be used in exactly the same way as you would use felt pens. The only difference is that the surface has changed from paper to different types of icing, such as fondant, glacé or royal icing. Allow the icing on the cake to dry completely before applying the paintwork, otherwise the paintwork might run.

METHOD

1. Work out the chosen design on the cake using a food colouring pen or a pin.
2. Mix the colours on a plate or palette, using only a small amount of water – excessive water might cause the icing to dissolve slightly.
3. Effective shading can be achieved by using good paintbrushes and different strengths and combinations of food colouring. When the design is completely dry, you can use the food colouring pens to outline and define aspects of the design, for example facial features, writing or borders.

NOTE

Painting takes a little longer to dry on fondant icing than on royal icing.

Basic Moulded Daisy Bunches and Shapes

DAISIES

Ready-made daisies are available in cake icing shops, but you may make them at home if you wish.

INSTRUCTIONS

Use the following equipment:

1. Small rolling pin
2. Daisy cutter or plunger
3. Fine paintbrush
4. Stamens
5. Piece of foam rubber
6. Florist's wire and tape

INGREDIENTS

A little white vegetable fat

Fondant Icing (see page 11)

Royal Icing (see page 12) or egg white

METHOD

1. Using white vegetable fat, grease a smooth surface such as a marble or granite slab or a Formica surface.
2. Roll out the fondant icing thinly and, using the daisy cutter or plunger, cut out about 10 daisies.
3. Dry daisies flat and top with a dot of royal icing in the centre, or brush the centre with egg white and pierce

with the stamen stem. Thread the stem through until the stamen rests against the flower (see illustration).

4. Cup the flower slightly around the stamen and leave to dry on a piece of foam rubber.
5. When dry, group daisies in bunches. Stagger heights and bind stems with florist's wire and tape for easy handling. Using a skewer or modelling tool, make a hole in the icing and insert the stems into the cake.

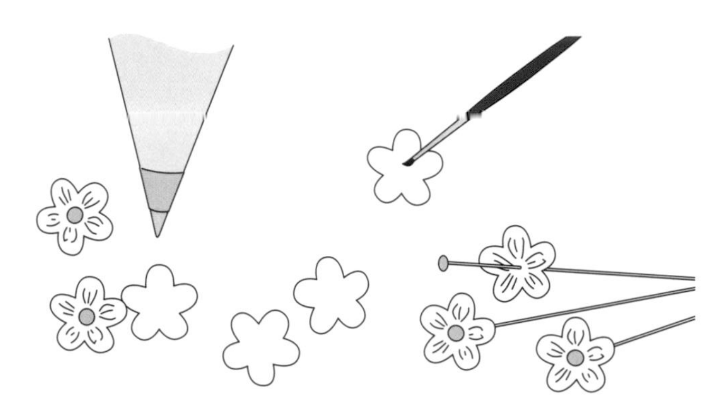

LEAVES AND OTHER FLAT SHAPES

1. Roll out the fondant icing on a flat surface that has been greased with white vegetable fat. Using cutters (such as biscuit cutters) or a sharp knife, cut out the required shapes.
2. Leaves can easily be decorated by using a skewer or any other blunt object to mark the veining. You can dry the leaves either flat or curled to make them look as natural as possible.

MODELLED SHAPES

Fondant icing can be used to model just about any shape you may require. It can be coloured either by kneading the food colouring into the dough before shaping, or by applying the food colouring with a paintbrush once the modelled shape is dry.

Sugar Crystal Decorations

This technique can be used for decorations such as the bell of a fire engine, or for moulded shapes to attach to the sides of a cake.

INSTRUCTIONS

Have the plastic moulds ready for use.

INGREDIENTS

60 ml (60 g, 2 oz, 4 tbsp) caster sugar

5 ml (1 tsp) egg white

Edible liquid food colouring (optional)

METHOD

1. Place the caster sugar in a bowl and, using a fork, gradually stir in a few drops of the egg white until the sugar resembles damp sand.
2. Colour the sugar if necessary, and then press firmly into plastic moulds.
3. Invert the plastic moulds on a flat tray and tap very gently to release the forms.
4. Leave the sugar crystal decoration in a warm, dry place to set completely.

NOTES

1. *When making the sugar bells, leave them to dry until the sugar has set slightly, forming a dry crust on the outside of the bell.*
2. *Place the bell back into the plastic mould and, using a skewer, gently scoop out the sugar in the centre so that you leave a hollow shape.*
3. *Remove the plastic mould and leave the sugar bells to harden completely.*

Chocolate Decorating

MOULDED CHOCOLATE DECORATIONS

INSTRUCTIONS

1. Have the plastic moulds ready for use.
2. Prepare the piping bag (see page 75).

INGREDIENTS

Melted cooking chocolate

Food colouring powder (for colouring white chocolate)

METHOD

1. Break up the chocolate and melt it gently, either in a heatproof bowl over simmering water, while stirring occasionally, or in a microwave oven in a covered glass bowl or jug on a very low heat setting for about 2 minutes. Stir well to remove all lumps. (Do not over-heat chocolate when melting it, as it will spoil and you will have to start again with fresh chocolate.)
2. Colour the melted white chocolate with food colouring powder only. If filling small plastic moulds, pour the chocolate into a piping bag. (You have more control when using a piping bag, resulting in less mess and waste.) For large plastic moulds, for example the owl and pussycat moulds, pour chocolate into the mould directly from the bowl or jug in which it was melted.
3. For small plastic moulds, snip off the tip of the piping bag and pipe the melted chocolate into the moulds.
4. When completely firm, remove from the mould.
5. Store the chocolate decorations between layers of non-stick baking paper in a sealed container in a cool place until ready to use.

DECORATING MOULDED CHOCOLATE SHAPES

This type of decorating can be done using piped melted chocolate, as in the bees on the beehive cake, or by paint-work using food colouring powders mixed with a non-toxic base, as in the owl and the pussycat chocolate shapes.

NOTE

Remember to clean your brushes! Use the special non-toxic cleaning solvent that can be obtained with the non-toxic base and food colouring at cake icing shops.

CHOCOLATE FLOODWORK

INGREDIENTS AND EQUIPMENT

Melted chocolate in two or more shades

2 or more substitute or disposable piping bags

Fine paintbrush

METHOD

1. Trace or draw the shape you require onto the reverse side of a piece of non-stick baking paper. Place the paper right side up on a flat surface, for instance a wooden board.
2. Melt the chocolate (see step 1 of Moulded Chocolate Decorations on this page) to be used for the outline and then fill the piping bag without removing its tip. Just before you start piping around the outside edge, snip off as much of the tip as is required for the thickness of the outline.
3. When the chocolate outline has set completely, melt the contrasting coloured chocolate and then flood the centre of the shape, using the other piping bag (or bags, depending on how many colours are being used). Remove the tip of the bag only just before flooding the outlined area.
4. Start by flooding the areas furthest away from you, keeping as close as possible to the chocolate outline without touching it with the piping bag.
5. Keep the piping bag close to the surface of the paper, thereby reducing the formation of air bubbles, and move it backwards and forwards across the shape.
6. When the design is almost filled, use a small paint-brush to brush the melted chocolate to the outline to create a smooth edge. If any bubbles appear, remove

them with the tip of a skewer or pin before chocolate sets. Once the chocolate floodwork shapes have set, remove them from the non-stick baking paper using a palette knife, and decorate and store as for moulded chocolate decorations (see page 81).

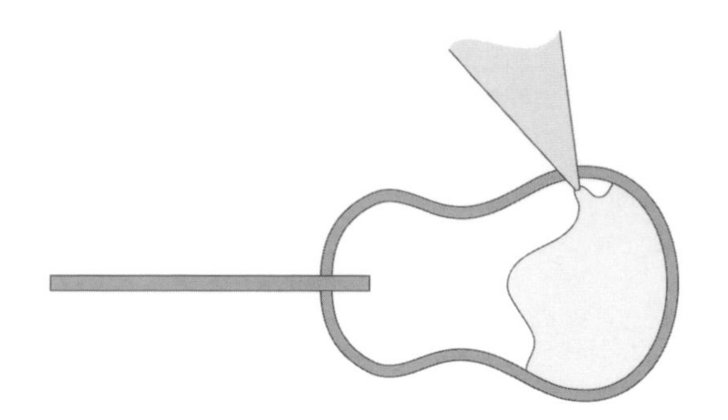

Using Candy and Sweets for Decorating

These decorations add so much excitement and fun to a birthday cake and can be very practical when one considers the variety of shapes and types of sweets available. For example, it is far easier and tastier to use a jelly dolphin sweet or gum than to mould one in fondant icing. Once the style of birthday cake has been established, a visit to a sweet shop should be very helpful. When attaching sweets to wet icings like royal, glacé or butter icings, be careful to choose sweets of which the colours will not run. Sweets such as Smarties or M & M's are ideal when attached with melted dark chocolate or used on chocolate icing for decorating.

Ideal sweets for decorating include:

1. **Fizz bars** – These bars must only be removed from their paper covering just before curling. Place the wrapped Fizz bar on a Pyrex dish in the oven's warming drawer. Put the heat on a low setting. After a few minutes, remove Fizz bars from the warming drawer. Take off the wrappers and curl the bars as desired. Use immediately or place the bars in the refrigerator so that they hold their shapes.
2. **Chocolate Flake** – These are useful for logs, tree bark and verandah pillars. They can also be used to strengthen and support moulded cakes, for example the ice-cream Dalmatian cake, where it is necessary to insert a chocolate Flake through the pup's neck to keep the head in place.
3. **Chocolate Matchmakers** in various flavours (e.g. mint, orange, coffee, etc.) **or Choc Stix** – These sticks have many uses, for instance ladders, poles (playground equipment and masts supporting rice paper sails on boats), fences, logs, window frames and doors. Attach them with cooled melted chocolate, which sticks more quickly than warm chocolate.
4. **Liquorice** – A lot of liquorice has been used in this book, because it is available in so many shapes and forms. It has been used for the cannons, the fire engine's water pipes and wheels, and on the space shuttle. Liquorice All-sorts are invaluable on children's cakes, whether they are whole or sliced. They can be used for windows, sills, eyes, wheels, etc.
5. **Jelly Tots** – These sweets provide you with a wide variety of wonderful colours that you can use to enliven the edging on a roof, for tree lights, etc.

Other useful sweets are jellybeans, chocolate buttons, candy bars, sour candy straws, candy belts, lollipops and marshmallows. In addition, sweets can be combined to make flower decorations on cakes, for example:

MARSHMALLOW FLOWERS

1. Using scissors, slice marshmallows into 5–6 petals.
2. Overlay the petals to form a flower.
3. Place a round sweet in the centre of each flower where the petals overlap. Because cut marshmallow is sticky, the petals and sweet will stick in position.

ICE-CREAM HORSE
(¼ SIZE)

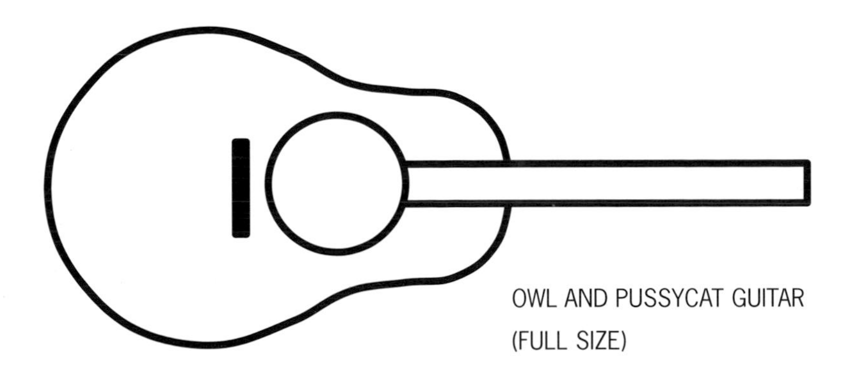

OWL AND PUSSYCAT GUITAR
(FULL SIZE)

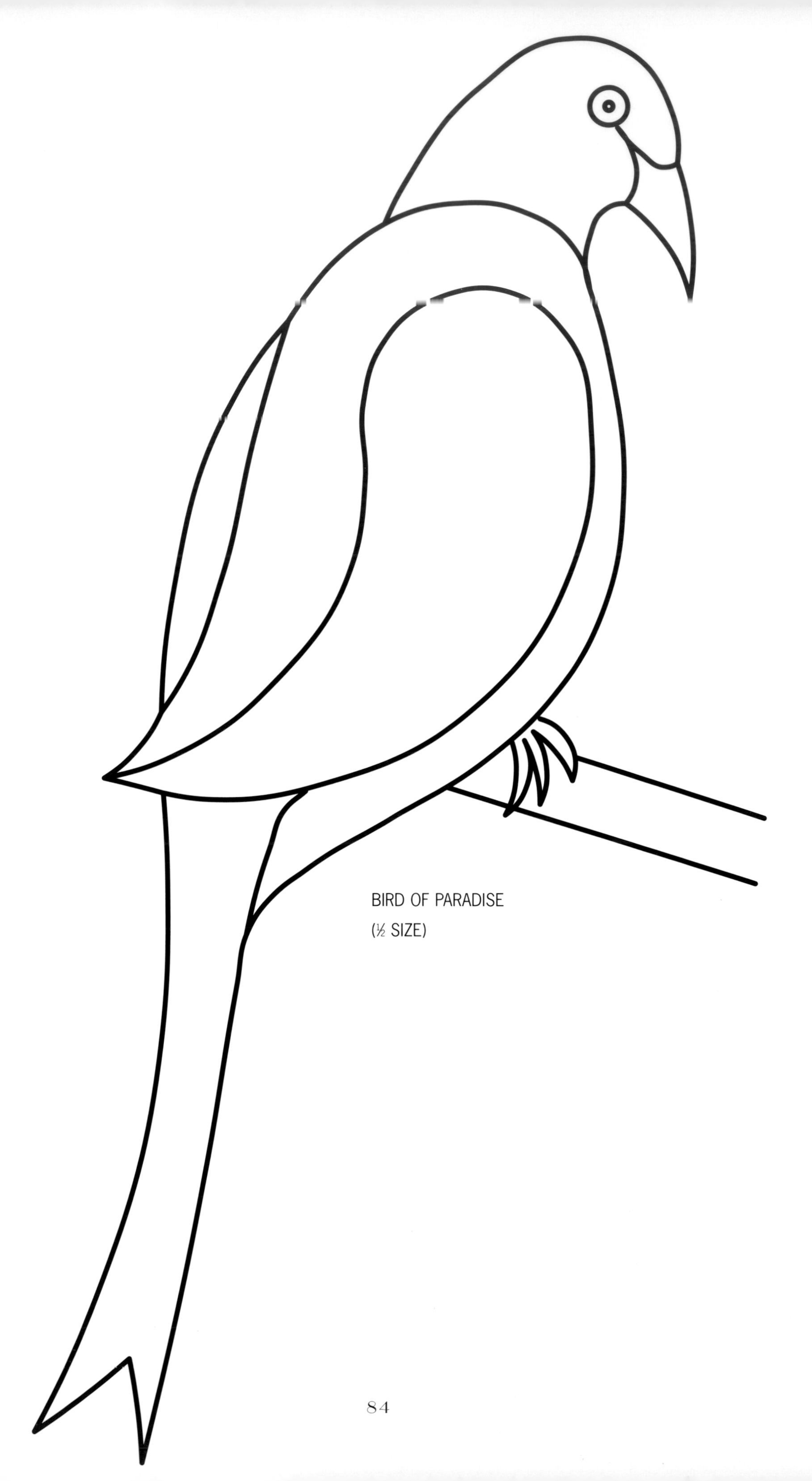

BIRD OF PARADISE
(½ SIZE)

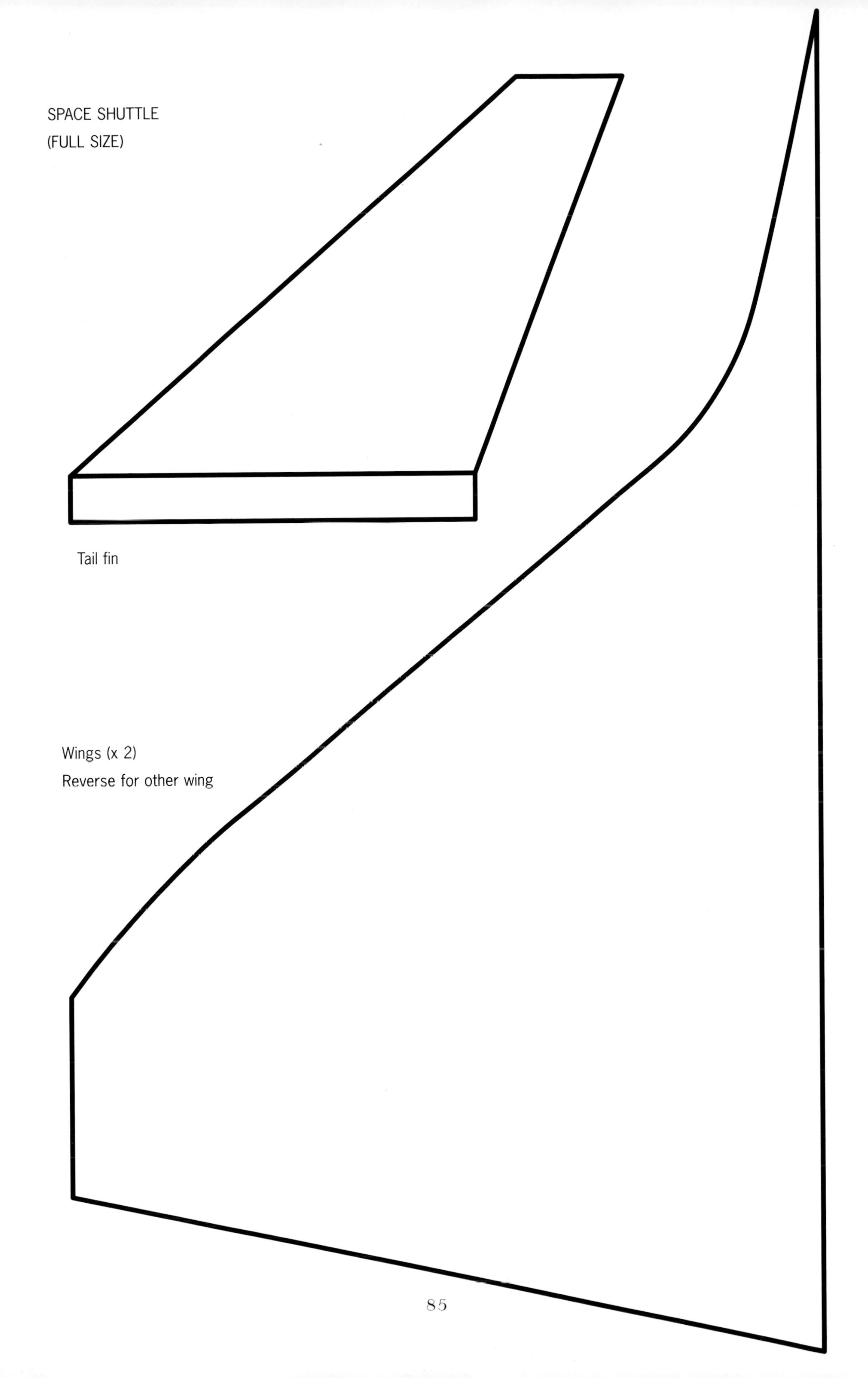
SPACE SHUTTLE
(FULL SIZE)
Tail fin
Wings (x 2)
Reverse for other wing

CHRISTMAS TREE
(½ SIZE)
HALF SUNFLOWER

QUEEN OF HEARTS
(½ SIZE)

Index